LOVE
MERCY &
GRACE

LOVE
MERCY &
GRACE

TRUE STORIES OF
GOD'S AMAZING CARE

COMPILED BY **KEREN BALTZER**

Guideposts

New York

Love, Mercy & Grace

ISBN-10: 0-8249-3432-6
ISBN-13: 978-0-8249-3432-3

Published by Guideposts
16 East 34th Street
New York, New York 10016
Guideposts.org

Distributed by Ideals Publications, a Guideposts company
2630 Elm Hill Pike, Suite 100
Nashville, Tennessee 37214

Guideposts and *Ideals* are registered trademarks of Guideposts.

Acknowledgments

Every attempt has been made to credit the sources of copyrighted material used in this book. If any such acknowledgment has been inadvertently omitted or miscredited, receipt of such information would be appreciated.

Scripture quotations marked (NIV) are taken from *The Holy Bible, New International Version.* Copyright © 1973, 1978, 1984, 2011 by Biblica, Inc. Used by permission of Zondervan. All rights reserved worldwide. www.zondervan.com

Scripture quotations marked (RSV) are taken from the *Revised Standard Version of the Bible.* Copyright © 1946, 1952, 1971 by Division of Christian Education of the National Council of Churches of Christ in the United States of America. Used by permission.

Scripture quotations marked (TLB) are taken from *The Living Bible.* Copyright © 1971 by Tyndale House Publishers, Wheaton, Illinois 60187. All rights reserved.

Library of Congress Cataloging-in-Publication Data has been applied for.

Cover and interior design by Müllerhaus
Cover photograph by iStock
Typeset by Aptara, Inc.

Printed and bound in the United States of America
10 9 8 7 6 5 4 3 2 1

Contents

Introduction

God's love for His children is profound, His mercy unending, His grace boundless. But sometimes it's all too easy to let the doubts creep in. Could God really care for *me*? When troubles crash in, we wonder where God is. When we've done wrong, we feel unworthy of His kindness and forgiveness.

Yet we are assured in Scripture, "I have loved you with an everlasting love; I have drawn you with an unfailing kindness" (Jeremiah 31:3 NIV). The amazing thing is that God frequently chooses to reveal His love through other people, allowing them to be conduits of His mercy and grace.

In this compilation of stories, discover how God showed His love for ordinary people—often working through other ordinary people. May you be encouraged and uplifted as you see God move powerfully, pouring out His mercy and grace in awe-inspiring ways—and know that God longs to do the same for you!

LOVE MERCY & GRACE

The Boy I Could Never Forget

by Pauline Burgard

AFTER TWENTY YEARS AS A FULL-TIME WIFE AND MOTHER, I DECIDED NOW THAT MY KIDS WERE GROWN, I NEEDED A PART-TIME JOB TO KEEP ME BUSY. THE QUESTION WAS: WHAT EXACTLY COULD I DO?

Secretarial work was out—I couldn't take shorthand, and I typed at a snail's pace. I cooked for a husband and children, but that wasn't enough to prepare me for a job in any of the restaurants near my home in Kansas City, Missouri. What was I qualified for?

The answer came one day as I drove past a lot full of school buses. I pulled over to the side of the road. *That's it!* I thought. I loved kids, plus I'd put plenty of miles on our family Chevy.

First I had to pass a written test for my chauffeur's license. Then I began driving practice. The bus was enormous. I could turn, shift, brake, accelerate, but I could not get the huge thing into reverse. When my husband asked how my training was going, I told him, "Fine, as long as no kid lives on a dead-end street."

Please, Lord, I prayed, *help me drive the bus.*

By the time school started that year, I'd gotten the hang of it. I was happy in my new work. I became a combination chauffeur, nurse, and friend. And if the kids needed it, I'd put on my "Tough Big Sister" act. It was a lot like my previous job—being a mom.

When I think about my years of bus driving, I remember the snowstorms that seemed to start on Thanksgiving and last through March. I remember Christmases when I was presented with hundreds of "I love you, Polly" cards. I remember hearing "Itsy-Bitsy Spider" sung over and over until I heard it in my sleep. Mostly, though, I remember Charlie.

Charlie began riding my bus in September of my fourth year driving. Eight years old, with blond hair and crystalline gray eyes, he got on with a group of children. They all had stories to tell me about their summers. Charlie, though, ignored me. He didn't even answer when I asked his name.

From that day on, Charlie was a challenge. If a fight broke out, I didn't have to turn my head to know who had started it. If someone was throwing spitballs, I could guess the culprit's name. If a girl was crying, chances were Charlie had pulled her hair. No matter how I spoke to him, gently or firmly, he wouldn't say a word. He'd just stare at me with those big gray eyes of his.

I asked around some and found out Charlie's father was dead, and he didn't live with his mother. *He deserves my patience*, I thought. So I practiced every bit of patience I could muster. To my cheery "Good morning," he was silent. When I wished him a happy Halloween, he sneered. Many, many times I asked God how I could reach Charlie. "I'm at my wit's end," I'd say. Still, I was sure that this child needed to feel some warmth from me. So, when he'd pass by, I'd ruffle his hair or pat him on the arm.

Toward the end of that year, the kids on my bus gave me a small trophy inscribed "To the Best Bus Driver Ever." I propped it up on the dashboard. On top, I hung a small tin heart that a little girl had given me. In red paint she had written, *I love Polly and Polly loves me.*

On the next-to-last day of school I was delayed a few minutes talking to the principal. When I got on the bus, I realized that the tin heart was gone. "Does anyone know what happened to the little heart that was up here?" I asked. For once, with thirty-nine children, there was silence.

One boy piped up, "Charlie was the first one on the bus. I bet he took it."

Other children joined the chorus, "Yeah! Charlie did it! Search him!"

I asked Charlie, "Have you seen the heart?"

"I don't know what you're talking about," he protested. Standing up, he took a few pennies and a small ball out of his pockets. "See, I don't have it."

"I bet he does!" insisted the girl who had given me the heart. "Check his pockets."

Charlie glowered when I asked him to come forward. His gaze burned into mine. I stuck my hand into one pocket. Nothing. I reached into the other pocket. Then I felt it—the familiar outline of the small tin heart. Charlie stared at me for a long time. There were no tears in those big gray eyes, no plea for mercy. He seemed to be waiting for what he'd come to expect from the world. I was about to pull the tin heart out of Charlie's pocket when I stopped myself. *Let him keep it*, a voice seemed to whisper.

"It must have fallen off before I got here," I said to the kids. "I'll probably find it back at the bus depot." Without a word, Charlie returned to his seat. When he got off at his stop, he didn't so much as glance at me.

That summer Charlie moved away. The next school year, and every one thereafter, my bus was filled with new kids, some difficult, some delightful, all of them engaging. I remember the six-year-old girl who'd wet her pants with maddening regularity every Friday afternoon. I remember my horror when one of my riders was struck by a car whose driver had ignored the flashing bus lights. I knelt by the dazed child, holding him still to prevent further damage to his broken leg. And every spring there was a tornado warning, when I'd promise the kids I'd get them home safely.

Later, my husband and I bought our own small fleet of school buses, and I had more children under my care. Maybe because of my failure with Charlie, I worked extra hard to reach out to each one.

Eventually I retired. And there my story as a school bus driver ends, except for one more incident. A dozen years after retirement I was in a department store in Kansas City, when someone said tentatively, "Polly?"

I turned to see a balding man who was approaching middle age. "Yes?"

His face didn't look familiar until I noticed his big gray eyes. There was no doubt. It was Charlie.

He told me he was living in Montana and doing well. Then, to my surprise, he hugged me. After he let go, he pulled something from his pocket and held it up for me to see. An old key chain…bent out of shape, the lettering faded. You can probably guess what it was—the little tin heart that said, *I love Polly and Polly loves me.*

"You were the only one who kept trying," he explained. We hugged again and went our separate ways. That night, I thought over his words. *You were the only one who kept trying.* Of course, someone else kept trying too—and not just with Charlie. Before I fell asleep, I thanked the Lord for the reassurance that I'd done a good job and for all the qualifications He'd given me to do it with.

A Man Transformed
by Paul Everett

I'VE TAKEN ON SOME UNUSUAL PROJECTS IN MY LIFE. I'VE WORKED AS A MADISON AVENUE ADVERTISING MAN AND AS A MERCHANT FOR MACY'S, AFTER ALL. YET RECENTLY, IN MY SEVENTIES, I DID SOMETHING NO ONE—LEAST OF ALL, ME—WOULD HAVE EXPECTED. I WROTE A BOOK.

It started out with an innocent visit to a Franciscan hermitage in southwestern Pennsylvania, where I'd gone to still the spiritual restlessness I'd been feeling.

The monks all wore identical brown robes. Yet one stood out—a small, intense man with rugged good looks and an air of authority. That first day, he sat at the head of a table, long after the lunch dishes had been cleared, talking quietly to a rapt audience.

"That's Brother Jim," a priest told me. "He's been a powerful force here, ever since they let him out of jail."

Jail? But the priest offered no further explanation.

My next time at the monastery, I joined the group at Jim's table. He certainly had wit and warmth and told a good story, though that wasn't what drew people to him. It was a quality I can only describe as holiness, a quality as unmistakable as it is rare. God was at work in this man.

But what had he done to deserve time in prison? It must have been something minor. "I know Brother Jim does a lot of work at prisons," I said to Father Lester Knoll, the superior of the hermitage, one afternoon, "but did he really do time?"

Father Knoll looked at me intently. "Yes," he said. "It's public knowledge. He was away for twenty years."

A man doesn't go to prison for that long without having done something awful, perhaps even unforgivable.

"When Jim was twenty," Father Knoll explained, "he murdered his wife."

Murder? How does one go from being a murderer to being a monk? I believed in forgiveness and redemption. Still, to confront it so startlingly unnerved me. Yet I began to think of my own transformation, my own spiritual journey. Were Jim and I all that different?

I was twenty-seven years old and a new member of the team at Macy's department store at Herald Square in New York City. I was ambitious and driven. I'd pick up some merchandising experience at Macy's, then move back into the advertising field. A big salary would result.

Then my ambition stalled. I'd wake in the morning with no firm sense of myself. The goals I'd set—the ones that had driven me since I could remember—now felt like traps, as if the world were closing in on me just when it should have been opening up. I was depressed and scared, and I couldn't figure out why.

One day, I dragged myself into the office forty minutes late. My phone was ringing. It was the senior vice president. "Ellie Hummer wants to talk to you."

Ellie was the buyer for junior dresses. In just a few years, she'd built the department into a high-volume operation. She was tough, and everyone knew it. I'd done a little work with her myself—enough to be as much in awe of her as everyone else. But I had no idea why she needed to see me.

I went to Ellie's office. No Ellie. I waited, speculating about the chat she wanted to have with me. A new line of clothing? A brilliant marketing idea? Suddenly Ellie walked in. She told me she had indeed been thinking of using some of my services in her department. She also told me something else. "Paul, I've been praying for you."

I wasn't sure I'd heard right. "I'm sorry. Did you say praying?"

Ellie leaned forward and narrowed her eyes. "I've been watching you, Paul. There's something missing from your life. A plan. A plan that includes something bigger than you. A plan that includes the Lord."

That feeling that had been dogging me—was Ellie right? Was I feeling the absence of God in my life? It was as if a lens had been adjusted for me and my life had suddenly come into brilliant focus. At that instant, I knew not only that my life had been changed but that I had been fundamentally and forever transformed.

Kind as Ellie's offer was, I didn't end up taking it. Some time after our meeting, I announced to my astonished parents, "I need to find a way of living that includes God." Eventually I left the business world and commenced studies to become a minister.

By the time I met Jim, I'd been in the ministry for four decades. I believed that I'd done the work God wanted of me. Yet increasingly I felt as if He wasn't finished with me yet. It was that feeling that drew me back to the monastery, and Jim, month after month.

One day Father Knoll called me aside. "Paul, I'd like you to write Jim's story."

"You mean some kind of article?"

"No," he said. "A book. It will be a lot of work, and I can't pay you a cent. But I've prayed about this for a long time. You're the man who is supposed to tell his story."

I had no idea how to even begin such a huge undertaking. A book? People spend a lifetime writing just one. I was seventy-two. But a small voice interrupted my train of negative thinking. Hadn't I come to the hermitage for spiritual direction? Hadn't I sensed God had further plans for me?

"Okay," I said at last. "Fine. I'll do it."

I spent the next couple of years getting to know Jim, trying to turn him inside out and find out what drove him. His honesty was jarring, almost brutal, but without it we would have gone nowhere. He made no excuses. His was a childhood of horrible abuse. Then a young marriage to a girl no more educated in how to live than he was. A year into it, convinced she was drawing away from him, just as everyone else in his life always had, Jim was overcome by a moment of rage and violence. He lashed out and ended his life almost as surely as he ended his wife's.

In prison, he met a chaplain who told him his life wasn't over. God had a plan. With God, he would find a way through the guilt and horror of his past, and into the holy light of forgiveness. With God he could be free. But only with God.

Jim fought it. He wanted no part of God or religion or the Bible. But the chaplain had gotten through, and that meeting was the beginning of Jim's new life, much as the meeting with Ellie was the beginning of mine.

Now my journey had taken another twist, and I found myself doubting if I could write a book, doubting if I could do what God was asking. But does He ever ask of us what we cannot do?

Jim and I had both been prisoners. Our sins were different, but the distance we'd kept from God wasn't. That distance was measured in the absence of grace. That grace, when we allowed it into our lives, was transforming. It could transform anyone into anything, from a murderer to a monk, or a marketer into a published author at the ripe old age of seventy-two. Grace is the key. It can unlock the door of any prison.

03.

Amazing Grace
by William R. Nesbitt

HER MUSCLES GREW TENSE, HER POSTURE RIGID. HER EYES WIDENED IN TERROR. "THOSE PEOPLE ARE AFTER ME—THEY'RE GOING TO KILL ME! I'M GOING TO DIE! I DON'T WANT TO DIE!" THEN SHE TURNED TO ME. "YOU HATE ME. I'M GOING TO KILL YOU AND I'M GOING TO KILL MYSELF!"

My wife, Bernice, whom I have loved for almost half a century, was having delusions and hallucinations that were so real they were chilling.

As a physician I knew she had the terminal symptoms of vascular dementia, a disease that is always fatal and is almost indistinguishable from Alzheimer's disease, the illness from which her mother had died. She no longer remembered important people or events in her life. Even I was a stranger. To her, our marriage had never taken place, our children had never been born, and our nearly fifty happy years together had never existed. And the medication she was taking didn't seem to help.

Twenty-two and a half hours a day expressions of terror poured from her lips. She ran from room to room trying to escape the bizarre prison her deteriorating brain had created. Only sheer exhaustion permitted her an hour and a half of troubled sleep at night. I called a psychiatrist for another evaluation, and we arranged for her to be hospitalized.

Two years earlier, in 1993, she had been evaluated at Duke University's Memory Disorders Clinic. Numerous specialists had ordered every conceivable test. They confirmed the diagnosis of severe advanced dementia and recommended institutional care.

At the hospital in St. Helena, I gave the psychiatrist her extensive medical records. Together, Bernice and I walked down the corridor to the nurses' station. The blank expression on my wife's face belied the intensity of the fear I could sense by her tight grip on my hand. A nurse greeted us and told me, "We'll take good care of her," as she gently released Bernice's fingers from my hand.

Bernice said nothing, and I couldn't speak—not even to say good-bye. I gave Bernice a gentle hug before the nurse led her to her room. Then I hurried for the exit. Mists of sorrow were already blurring my vision.

I couldn't come to terms with what I had just done. I had left my wife in a locked psychiatric ward, and she didn't know why I had deserted her. I knew that in the dim recesses of her mind the tenuous shadows of reality told her she could depend on me—and I had taken that security from her.

As I left the hospital, high on a mountainside overlooking the Napa Valley, where the vineyards were being harvested, my storm clouds of despair erupted into a torrent of tears. Driving through the quiet serenity of that beautiful valley, I thought back to when I had first seen Bernice. She had been wearing a purple knit dress and was leading the church's college group. Her effervescent charm immediately captured my heart and I wanted her for my wife. I knew I could love her forever.

As our friendship grew and our marriage matured, I discovered why I loved her. I loved her for her spiritual strength, the warmth of her companionship, and her skills as mother and wife. I was proud of her professional accomplishments as a teacher and school administrator. But when her illness developed, those wonderful attributes were gradually stripped away.

Driving toward my empty home, I suddenly realized that those were selfish reasons for loving her. Now I loved her more than ever; not for what she could give to me, but for the love and care I could give her.

My prayers mingled with the rush of wind pouring through the car window. To me that wind seemed like the voice of God, whispering to me that Bernice was His special child and I should take care of her for Him.

Take care of her? Doubt and hopelessness enveloped me. I thought of her irrational behavior and the demands of her total dependency. I dreaded her frenetic activity, the incessant movement, her refusal even to sit long enough to eat. I had pursued her from room to room, spoon in hand, trying to get her to swallow a few bites. I had watched in despair as her once beautiful figure wasted away.

I had spent hours undoing the irrational tasks she felt compelled to do. Linens, clothes, silverware, and dishes disappeared, to be found in the most unexpected places. I had to put childproof latches on cupboards and closets and locked doors and disconnected potentially dangerous appliances. How could I cope with my inevitable exhaustion if I should take her back? Then I thought of our marriage vows. I had promised to take care of her in sickness and in health, and I had made those vows to God as well as to Bernice. With trepidation, I said, "Yes, Lord, with Your help I will take care of her." But I had to give the hospital time to stabilize her.

The next day the doctor called: "I'm sorry to tell you this, but your wife's behavior is so disruptive we had to put her in physical restraints. I have started her on two new powerful antipsychotic drugs that I am sure will calm her down." When I called two days later he said the restraints were no longer needed.

As each day went by, the emptiness in my life became more unbearable. By the fifth day I could no longer stand the separation. I went to get her.

The psychiatrist did not want to let her go. "She is not well regulated on her medication," he said. "She should stay a few days longer." Then he warned me, "Your wife is severely demented and needs constant supervision in a skilled nursing facility."

"I realize that," I answered.

I felt a surge of joy when Bernice grasped my hand and the trace of a smile brightened her face. A nurse's aide wheeled her to the exit and we started home.

But at home I was shocked by her condition. She was still severely psychotic. Her medicine had calmed her into a drugged apathy. She had lost even more weight. She was incontinent, her posture was stooped, her gait shuffling, and saliva dripped from her chin. She had the same appearance I had seen in people who were dying—sallow skin, shallow breathing, a listless response to outside stimuli, and a passive look of resignation that said, "The fight is over."

I prayed, "Dear Lord, not yet, not yet—give me one more chance." But to do what? I had already exhausted every medical option I knew of. Yet as I prayed, a strange idea flashed into my mind. God seemed to be telling me to stop all of her medications and give Him a chance.

"But, Lord, she will become uncontrollable again!" I said. Yet I knew I had to do it.

Over the next several weeks, I carefully tapered off all of her medicines. Tensely I watched as some of her agitation returned. But then, as the weeks went by, I noticed Bernice was getting better.

I have practiced general and family medicine, with a subspecialty in psychiatry, for more than fifty years. I did research for a major drug company on the treatment of dementia, and I've been the primary physician for hundreds of demented patients. I have never seen one sustain a long-term improvement. But God is not limited by a medical prognosis.

Nearly two years have gone by since I weaned Bernice from her medications, and the sparkle has returned to her eyes. Recently we sat in our breakfast room after a good night's sleep. The sun poured through the windows, a breeze rustled the leaves in the trees, and Bernice sat eating her breakfast—without help. She looked up at me, smiled, and said, "I love you. I am so happy."

She still has a long way to go, but every day the miracle continues—without regular medication. Each gain is not dramatic, just a small discovery of another recovered ability she had lost. She is no longer incontinent; she can dress herself and brush her teeth, and she tries to help with household tasks. Her cognitive function has improved.

Once again we can do some limited traveling and go out to eat in restaurants.

Bernice especially loves to go to church. She used to sing in the church choir, but because of her impaired memory and conversational ability I had not heard her sing a note for several years.

Last year I took Bernice to the noon Good Friday service. She sat quietly until the closing hymn, "Amazing Grace." Then, to my astonishment, she began to sing every word of that beautiful hymn from memory. When she reached the third verse, my spirits soared as she sang with dazzling assurance, "Through many dangers, toils and snares, I have already come; 'Tis grace hath brought me safe thus far, And grace will lead me home."

How right it was for her to be singing those words. Through her darkest days, with mind and memory gone, Bernice had held on to her faith with a divine tenacity. God's grace had brought her—and me—safe thus far, and I knew He would walk with us through whatever trials still lay ahead, to see us safely home.

04.

Not So Different After All

by Bob Massie

ONE OF THE MOST DIFFICULT THINGS ABOUT MY CHILDHOOD WAS THAT I OFTEN FELT ALONE. I KNEW THAT SOMEHOW I WAS DIFFERENT FROM MY FRIENDS, AND THAT DIDN'T BOTHER ME SO MUCH—I JUST COULDN'T UNDERSTAND WHY SOME CHILDREN TREATED BADLY SOMEONE WHO WAS DIFFERENT AND WHY SOME PARENTS WERE AFRAID TO LET THEIR CHILDREN VISIT ME. YOU SEE, I WAS BORN WITH A DISORDER THAT MEDICAL SCIENCE HAD YET TO FIND A CURE FOR—HEMOPHILIA. BUT SCIENCE HAD NOTHING TO DO WITH FINDING THE CURE FOR MY FEELING DIF-FERENT. IN MY SENIOR YEAR OF COLLEGE, I QUITE UNEXPECTEDLY FOUND THAT FOR MYSELF.

Perhaps the children were afraid because I wore leg braces on both my legs to help me walk. Perhaps the parents were concerned that their children might hit me and this would cause trouble. Even years later, when I was an active undergraduate at Princeton and no longer had to wear the leg braces, I had to spend a lot of time explaining hemophilia to my friends and roommates. Today I meet many people who still think that hemophilia is a disease where you could bleed to death from a cut.

Well, I can't bleed to death from a cut. This is only one of the many fallacies about the disease. Simply put, hemophilia is a chronic incurable blood disease caused by a missing protein that prevents the blood from clotting properly. Genetically transmitted by females and manifested only in males, hemophilia became known as the "disease of kings" in the nineteenth century when Queen Victoria of England, a carrier, passed the disease on to several male heirs to European thrones. I'm not related to royalty; in fact, hemophilia is pretty evenly distributed among all races and ethnic backgrounds. Until 1968, when I was twelve, most hemophiliacs regularly had to undergo transfusions of fresh frozen human plasma, usually at a hospital. Now the clotting protein, known as "factor VIII," has become available as an intravenous injection that can be administered by the hemophiliac at home.

There is a lot of pain. Periodic internal joint bleeding, most often in the ankles, knees, or elbows, can be excruciating. The long-term effect of this is joint deterioration and chronic arthritis. Every morning, I awake with my corroded leg joints stiff from arthritis that has set in during the night, and I must hobble to sit in a hot bath for fifteen minutes before I can walk. At Princeton I used a small electric cart to get around the big campus. Even now I have to be careful how far I walk.

The picture isn't totally grim. I was blessed with incredible parents who, with an inexhaustible supply of love and wisdom, brought me up in a home where self-pity melted and hope abounded.

When I was growing up in the Hudson River village of Irvington, New York, my illness was just an accepted part of our lives. Like any other kid, I remember good-natured scraps and pillow fights with my two younger sisters. And as for the leg braces, the wheelchair, and the middle-of-the-night trips to the hospital for transfusions—well, all of these were, in a strange way, no more unusual to our family than clothes to be washed or dishes to be dried.

I'm sure my condition was just as emotionally draining for my parents as it was for me—if not more so. And it was financially draining, too, especially since my parents were journalists on small salaries. Yet it was my illness that led my father, Robert Massie, to write his first book, *Nicholas and Alexandra*, about the last Russian tsar and tsarina who also had a son with hemophilia, Alexis. Books had been written about the imperial family before, but no one had ever examined the effect this illness had on the family and thus on the future of Russia. My mother (who helped with the research and editing) and father spent many hours comparing their own experiences as parents with those of the Russian royal family.

My mother became extremely interested in Russia, and because she was home taking care of me, she began taking regular classes in Russian at the local community college. The classes cost six dollars a semester—at that time barely all we could afford. Mom not only learned to speak fluent Russian but also became an authority on Russian art and culture.

Eventually my parents collaborated to write *Journey*, a candid account of their experiences as parents of a chronically ill child—a book that's now required reading in many medical and nursing schools.

When I was twelve, we went to live in Paris. We moved partly because of Dad's new book project and partly so that we could learn French. My health improved while I was there because the expensive factor VIII concentrate was available to me free (France has a national health program). We lived there for four years and then we came back home. In 1974, I started at Princeton.

Three years later, after my junior year as a history major, I was awarded a small research grant for three weeks of study in the archives of the French Foreign Ministry. And so, in the summer of 1977, I was back in Paris!

Like many college students, I was trying to figure out what was really important in life and what sort of career I should pursue. I began taking early-morning walks. The streets were gray and quiet, not unlike my mood. One Sunday I wandered into the American Church in Paris, which I had attended years before as a high school student. I hadn't been to church for a long time. Though in college I had been drawn to Princeton's chapel by its soaring beauty—often visiting there late at night for a few moments of solitude—I had never attended services.

On this particular Sunday morning far away from home, I found myself sitting in church again, and it somehow seemed...right.

Everything about the service, from the music to the minister's sermon, gripped me in a way nothing had for years. As I walked home, I felt a curious sort of anticipation about what the rest of the day would bring, as though I were about to embark on an adventure.

That afternoon I joined my cousin and some friends for a picnic at a house outside of Paris. Several of the people there described themselves as "Christians"—in fact, they made a deliberate point of it—and I was surprised when I found myself falling into a long discussion with a young woman named Windy. She seemed so confident about her faith that I wanted to shoot down some of her religious talk with a few hard-hitting questions. But the first thing I knew, Windy was asking me the questions and I was hard put to offer her anything more than the most feeble responses.

"Tell me, Bob," she said softly. "What does the word salvation mean to you? Do you think you will be with Jesus after you die?"

I'd always thought of myself as a Christian; that is, as long as I could remember, I'd always believed in Christ. I'd just never thought much about Him. Yet Windy called Him Jesus and seemed to know Him intimately.

"I don't know," I stammered in reply. "I mean, I hope that someday, somewhere, there's an afterlife. But my faith isn't very strong. I'm not really good enough. I can't believe that I deserve salvation."

"Deserve salvation?" Windy said. "Who on earth deserves salvation? That's a human idea—that we can earn salvation by being good. God loves us—loves you—unconditionally, in spite of all your failings, weaknesses, infirmities. Most people can't understand this concept of something for free, this gift of grace. The Bible explains it this way: 'Since all have sinned and fall short of the glory of God, they are justified by His grace as a gift, through the redemption which is in Christ Jesus'" (Romans 3:23–24 RSV).

Could it be true that God's love was bigger than the trials, pain, and suffering that are part of life? Bigger, even, than my struggles with hemophilia?

I met with Windy again a few days later, and this time I prayed with her.

The prayer was a simple one. I asked God to open my heart so that Jesus could come into my life in a new and meaningful way. There was no flash of light. No music. No apparitions. I said good-bye to Windy. I returned home to the United States, to school. Nothing was changed.

Yet something was different.

I felt more at peace, more settled. As a result, my senior year of college was unlike any other: a year of wonder, accomplishment, and growth. This new relationship with God focused my attention on deeper thoughts and questions and gave me greater courage to speak up about problems I saw around me. I worried less about what others thought of my hemophilia, or of my faith. Still, I longed to have a group of people to talk to about this new presence in my life.

No one was more surprised than I when my growing interest in Christianity led me to Yale Divinity School. There, I started to sense a link between my experiences with hemophilia and my faith, a link forged by the direct and unsentimental way Christianity deals with human suffering. I came to believe that God doesn't cause tragedies. These things are part of the human condition, arising from our own sinfulness, the darkness of chaos, or meaningless chance. However, God does have the power to redeem the bad things in life and even use them to His glory.

That all made perfect sense to me—I believed it—but I still felt "different." And I wondered how God could use something as complicated and painful as hemophilia.

The answer wasn't long in coming. I was soon assigned to be a hospital chaplain in New Haven. As I sat by the bedsides of patients— ill, frightened, in pain—I felt a special kinship to them. I had been in their position and might be again. In that place, I was not different.

After graduation, I was called to be an Episcopal priest in New York City. There I witnessed something even more startling. I met an enormous variety of people—students, businesspeople, artists, clergy, actors. I found that everyone, from the poorest street person to the most affluent parishioner, from people of deep religious faith to people with no faith at all, had known suffering. Everyone. One person loses a brother; another, a child; a third is consumed by guilt; a fourth, by disease. No one is exempt, not even God. His own Son, Jesus Christ, died an agonizing death. Far from being the most isolating experience in life, suffering is one of the few universal experiences that bind us truly and tightly together.

Having worried so long about being "different" from others, I find it incredible that my hemophilia, which I had thought set me apart, has turned out to be the very thing that gives me common ground with everyone I meet!

In this life, if I can offer anything to anyone who is lonely or in pain or in doubt, it is only because through hemophilia I have known these things myself. God, through the power of His Son, has transformed my illness from my greatest weakness into my greatest strength.

05.

A Lesson Warmly Taught

by Jill Taylor

WHEN I WAS A TEENAGER, MY PARENTS WERE OFTEN WORRIED AND EXASPERATED BY MY FAILURE TO GET HOME ON TIME AFTER DATES. AND I DIDN'T TRY REALLY HARD TO MEET THEIR CURFEWS UNTIL I FOUND A COMPELLING REASON ONE COLD WINTER NIGHT.

"Be sure you're home by midnight," my mother told me as my boyfriend and I left the house. We were going to hear one of the big bands at a dance hall fifty miles away. The music was terrific, and we stayed later than we should have. Then, coming home, we were slowed by a highway accident.

I began to picture the angry scene my lateness would provoke. "Oh, I dread this," I moaned to my date. "The minute I get home my mother'll lace into me. She'll be waiting right at the door."

But she wasn't. She'd gone to bed, leaving some lights on for me. I tiptoed guiltily to my own room. The confrontation would come tomorrow.

Shivering in the chilly air, I undressed quickly and slipped between the icy sheets. What a surprise! Instead of coldness, I found a pocket of warmth, Under the covers at the foot of the bed, my mother had tucked a toasty-warm hot-water bottle. Oh, how good it felt!

As I snuggled deeper, pressing my feet against the welcome heat, I felt enveloped in security and warmth. Rather than scolding, my mother had chosen this way to show how much she loved me and cared what happened to me.

I said my prayers gratefully, and then, still basking in my mother's kindness, I thought of Jesus. So often He showed His love for someone even when He didn't approve of that person's actions. Mother was following the lead of the gentlest Teacher the world has ever known.

Suddenly, intensely, I didn't want to disappoint my mother with my laxity and lateness anymore.

And you know what? I didn't!

06.

I Saw the Hand of God Move

by Joe Stevenson

I'VE ALWAYS BELIEVED IN GOD. BUT OVER THE YEARS MY BELIEFS ABOUT WHO GOD IS—AND WHAT HE CAN DO—HAVE CHANGED. IT WASN'T UNTIL MY SON WAS GRAVELY ILL THAT I LEARNED YOU CAN BELIEVE IN GOD AND YET NOT KNOW HIM AT ALL.

Know. Knowledge. Logic. When I was younger, those were the words I wanted to live by. As a child I contracted scarlet fever, and this illness ruled out my ever playing sports or roughhousing around. The only real adventures I could go on were adventures of the mind. I read books with a vengeance—Great Books of the Western World, and the volumes of Will and Ariel Durant, and literally thousands more—and out of my reading I formed my strongest beliefs. I believed in logic, in the mind's ability to put all creation into neat, rational categories.

At the same time I was growing up in a strongly Christian family, and so I believed in God. But I insisted—and my insistence caused a lot of arguments that God Himself was also a Being bound by logic and His own natural laws. I guess I pictured God as a great scientist. Miracles? No, God couldn't and wouldn't break laws in that way. When my family told me that Christianity means faith in a loving, miraculous God, I turned away and went looking for other religions—ones that respected the rational mind above all.

As I became a man, my belief in rationality helped me in my career. I became a salesman for the Bell System, and when I needed to formulate sales strategies and targets, logic unlocked a lot of doors on the way to success.

But other doors seemed to be closed. I felt dry, spiritually empty, and anxious. I tried meditation, ESP, and so on, but the emptiness increased to despair.

In utter defeat, I turned to God in prayer. His Spirit answered with, "I don't simply want belief that I exist. I want you, your will, your life, your dreams, your goals, your very being. And I want your faith, faith that I am sufficient for all your needs." My despair overcame my logic and I yielded all to Him. But just saying you have faith is not the same as having it. In my mind, I still had God in a box.

Maybe that's why I never thought to pray when my oldest son, Frank, came home from first grade one day and said he didn't feel well. What would God care about stomach flu?

A doctor whom my wife, Janice, and I had consulted wasn't very alarmed about Frank's illness at first. "It's really not too serious," the doctor assured us, "just a bad case of the flu complicated by a little acidosis. Give him this medicine and in a few days he'll be fine."

But Frank wasn't fine, not at all. The medicine worked for a day or so, but then his symptoms—the gagging, choking, and vomiting—came back more violently. His small, six-year-old frame was bathed in sweat and racked with convulsions. We checked him into the local hospital for further testing, but later in the evening our doctor said the original diagnosis was correct. "He's just got a real bad case of it," we were told.

I went to work the next day fully expecting to take Frank and Janice home that night, but when I stopped at the hospital to pick them up, our doctor was there to meet me. "I'd like to have a word with you two," he said, showing Janice and me into a private room.

"A problem, doctor?" I asked.

"Further testing has shown our previous diagnosis was incorrect. We think your son has acute nephritis. It's a terminal kidney disease . . ."

He paused, and I could feel the blood running from my face. "But we've found that in children there's a good chance of recovery. Your son has a ninety percent chance of being as good as new."

But by ten o'clock the next morning, the news was worse. Sometime during the night, Frank's kidneys had failed. Janice and I rushed to the hospital again.

"X-rays show Frank's kidneys are so badly infected that no fluid will pass through them," we were told. "The odds aren't in his favor anymore. If those kidneys don't start working within forty-eight hours, I'm afraid your son will die."

I looked at Janice, watching the tears well in her eyes as a huge lump formed in my throat. I took her hand in mine, and we slowly walked back to Frank's room. We were too shocked, too upset to even talk. All afternoon we sat at Frank's bedside, watching, stroking his matted blond hair, wiping his damp forehead. The stillness of the room was broken only by the beeps and blips of the machines monitoring little Frank's condition. Specialists would occasionally come, adjust a few tubes, make some marks on Frank's chart, and then silently go. I searched their eyes for an answer, for some glimmer of hope, and got nothing. When our minister came to pray for our son, I could only cry in desperation.

Late that evening, after Frank was asleep, we went home. Friends were waiting with a hot meal, words of encouragement, and news of a vast prayer chain they had begun. And for a fleeting moment, I thought I saw in Janice's eyes the spark of hope that I had been looking for from the doctors all afternoon.

By the following morning, that spark of hope had ignited a flame of confidence in Janice. "I turned Frank's life over to God last night," she told me excitedly, before we were even out of bed. "I feel a real peace about what's going to happen, that God's will is going to be done."

"God's will?" I said angrily. "What kind of God makes little boys get sick? He doesn't care!" And I rolled over. Peace? God's will? No, little Frank would need more than that to get well.

But my anger didn't stop me from trying to reason with God. All that morning, while Janice kept a hospital vigil, I begged and pleaded and screamed at God, daring Him to disprove my skepticism, trying to goad Him into action.

"Who do You think You are?" I shouted once. "Why are You doing this to my son? He's only six! Everybody says You're such a loving God—why don't You show it?" I yelled until I was exhausted. Finally, convinced my arguments were falling on deaf ears, I took our other children to a neighbor and headed to the hospital, thinking this might be the last time I'd see my son alive.

I never arrived; at least, a part of me didn't. In the car on the way, this Higher Being, this remote Power, this unjust God, spoke to me through His Spirit. I felt His presence soothing my still-hot anger. And I heard His voice, gentle, reassuring. He reminded me that I had made a commitment to Him, that I had promised to trust Him with my life, my all. And He had promised to take care of me, in all circumstances. "Take Me out of the box you've put Me in," He said, "and let Me work." By the time I parked the car, my heart was beating wildly. I sat for a few moments longer and uttered but two words in reply to all that had happened: "Forgive me."

By the time I reached Frank's room, I knew what I needed to do as clearly as if someone had given me written instructions. There had been no change in Frank's condition, so I sent Janice home to get some rest. Then I walked over to Frank's bed. Placing shaking hands where I thought his kidneys should be, I prayed as I never believed I would ever pray. "God, forgive me for my ego, for trying to make You what I want You to be. If You will, heal my son, and if You won't, that's all right too. I'll trust You. But, please, do either right now, I pray in Christ's name. Amen."

That was all. There were no lightning flashes, no glows, no surges of emotion like the rushing wind, only the blip-blip-blip of monitors. I calmly sat down in a chair, picked up a magazine, and began to wait for God's answer. There was only one difference. For the first time in my life, I knew I was going to get one.

Within moments, my eyes were drawn from the magazine to a catheter tube leading from Frank's frail-looking body. That tube was supposed to drain fluid from his kidneys, but for nearly two days it had been perfectly dry, meaning Frank's kidneys weren't working at all. But when I looked closely at the top of the tube, I saw a small drop of clear fluid forming. Ever so slowly it expanded, like a drop of water forming on the head of a leaky faucet, until it became heavy enough to run down the tube and into the collecting jar.

This was the most wonderful thing I had ever seen—the hand of God, working. I watched the tube, transfixed, fully expecting to see another drop of fluid form. In about two minutes, I did. Soon, the drops were coming regularly, about a minute apart. With every drip, I could hear God saying to me, "I am, and I care."

When the nurse came in on her regular half-hour rounds, she could barely contain her excitement. "Do you see this, do you see this?" she shouted, pointing to the collecting jar. "Do you know that this is more fluid than your son has excreted in the past forty-eight hours combined?" She grabbed the catheter and raised it, saying she wanted to get every drop, then rushed off.

Within minutes she was back. Grabbing a chair, she sat down next to me and, excitedly, we watched drops of fluid run down the tube. We were both awed at what was happening; for half an hour we murmured only short sentences. "Isn't God good?" she asked me at one point, and I nodded. When she finally got up to call the doctor, I went to call Janice.

An hour and a half later one of the specialists assigned to Frank's case arrived. Taking one look at the collector, he told us that it was a false alarm, that the fluid was too clear. Anything coming from a kidney as infected as Frank's was would be rust-colored and filled with pus. No, he said, the fluid had to be coming from somewhere else. But I knew—Frank was well again.

By the next morning more than five hundred centimeters of the clear fluid had passed into the collector, and it continued as the doctors ran tests and X-rays to try to determine its origin. Finally, two days later, our doctor called us into his office.

"Joe, Janice, I think we've been privileged to witness an act of God. All the X-rays taken in the last two days not only show no kidney infection, they show no sign that there was ever an infection. Frank's blood pressure and blood poison levels have also dropped suddenly…It is a definite miracle."

And this time I wasn't about to argue. At last, I fully believed in a God Whose love knows no bounds—not the bounds of logic, not the hold of natural laws. Faith. That's what I now had—that and the knowledge that one's belief in God is essentially hollow if the belief isn't founded on faith.

07.

From the Mouths of Babes

by Sue Monk Kidd

HE STANDS ON THE SIDEWALK BESIDE THE FRONT DOOR OF THE DEPARTMENT STORE LIKE AN OLD CIGAR-STORE INDIAN—A TALL, MOTIONLESS MAN WEARING NO EXPRESSION ON HIS FACE, ONLY SUNGLASSES. HE CLUTCHES A CIGAR BOX, WHICH HE THRUSTS OUT IN A GESTURE OF GREETING AND HOPE WHEN FOOTSTEPS COME HIS WAY. THE BOX RATTLES, THE FEET HURRY BY, AND HIS ARM SINKS BACK AGAINST HIS SEEMINGLY WOODEN BODY.

As my seven-year-old daughter and I approach the door, I notice her steps slowing. She has caught sight of him. I've seen him on the streets before. But this is her first encounter with a beggar. She seems transfixed by the sight.

"What's he doing?" she asks too loudly.

"He's asking for money," I whisper.

Then comes the eternal question. "Why?"

"Because he's poor and he needs help," I say, hoping that satisfies her.

As we draw beside him, the cigar box is thrust in our direction. Ann stops and peeps inside it. I grab her hand and pull her through the door.

As I'm browsing in the store, Ann wanders off. I quickly follow her to the front door where she's peering through the glass at the beggar.

"Mama, can we give him some money?" she asks, her eyes reflecting both sadness and hope.

"Well...sure we can." I snap open my purse. She peeps inside it just as she did with the cigar box. All I have is a dollar bill and two quarters.

I hand her the quarters. She stares at the two coins for a moment as if there is something big and important going on inside her. Then she blurts it out. "Mama, give him the dollar, too, and I'll pay you back from my allowance."

Her words cut through all my distraction and unconcern, and they touch me deeply. There is a ring to them, a resonance that is unmistakable and piercing. I hand her the dollar. I watch her walk over to the beggar and gaze up into his blind face before she lays the money in his box.

I know it's one of those moments that will stay long in my memory. *Ann and the cigar-box beggar.* I suspect God is hidden in the little episode. I think it is His voice I heard sounding through my daughter. God's voice saying, "Give him the dollar, give him all you have and I'll pay you back in joy and growth." And that is a lesson I needed to hear just then—to help me grow more sensitive to the needs of those who wait expectantly on the edges of my world. To be less preoccupied and more responsive. More generous.

But the incident taught me more than that. It reminded me that we should always pay attention to the casual events that cross our days, and listen well to the words in the air about us. For God's voice can come in small and commonplace ways we're apt to miss. It can come in the language of a little girl and a beggar.

08.

Mrs. B. and Her Buttermilk Biscuits
by Idella Bodie

THE YEAR WAS 1948. IN OUR BLEAK APARTMENT—WORLD WAR II ARMY BARRACKS CONVERTED INTO EX-GI HOUSING—I PACED CONCRETE FLOORS WITH OUR INFANT DAUGHTER, SUSANNE. MY ARMS ACHED. NEEDLELIKE PAINS KNOTTED IN MY SHOULDERS AND SHOT UP MY NECK.

Through the large plate-glass windows on either end of the all-in-one living-dining-kitchen area, I looked out at a raw wind whipping leaves against the monotonous asphalt sheeting stretching over row after row of flat army-green housing units. Despair blanketed me like the oncoming winter evening.

Barely more than a year ago I had married Jim, an engineering student at the University of South Carolina. We were both twenty years old. Our plans included my working until he got through school, but an early pregnancy had curtailed that. I had always longed for a family, and I thanked God daily for our precious daughter, but I was weary in body, mind, and soul. I could feel my zest for life slipping away and I did not have the power to do anything about it.

Jim would be coming in soon from his off-school hours of selling shoes at a job he'd taken to supplement our income from the GI Bill. We would have our usual end-of-the-month dinner of grilled cheese sandwiches and applesauce before he hunched over his grueling academic studies.

At age twenty-one, we were broke (the birth of our baby had drained our meager savings) and bone-tired from wrestling with a colicky daughter until wee morning hours.

I had tried feeding our infant more often, feeding her fewer times, placing a warm water bottle on her little tummy, and every other bit of advice to calm the balled fists, screams, and painful squirming. But nothing worked except holding her close during the rhythm of walking and patting her supple back. That, however, took energy, and mine was draining away like dingy dishwater slurping from the kitchen sink.

Outside I saw Mrs. B., the manager of the apartments. She plodded against the blustery wind, her shapeless maroon coat billowing out behind her. Wisps of stiff gray hair fanned beneath the odd-looking felt hat she always wore.

Instinctively, I stepped back from the window so she wouldn't see me. I was in no mood for her buoyant chatter. Everyone knew she had the reputation for "talking the horns off a billy goat."

I moved through our long room toward the back window. In the dim shadows outside I could see black coal spilling from the bins hugging each apartment—coal dug from leftover piles at the old Columbia Army Air Base to be fed to our big cast-iron stoves for warmth and cooking.

"Oh, Lord," I breathed, "where are You? What's to become of us?"

As if in answer to my plea, a knocking at the other end of the room startled me. Still jostling and patting my fretting daughter, I answered the knock.

It was Mrs. B. with a telephone message. "Honey," she said through the door I held ajar with my free hand, "your husband just called. The car broke down and he didn't want you to worry about his lateness."

Oh no, not again! my mind screamed. And, feeling somewhat ashamed for not inviting Mrs. B. in, I thanked her and closed the door against the chilling gust.

I could see Jim shivering along the busy highway as he leaned under the hood of the used '36 Chevrolet. He would try to repair it himself—there was no money for the car.

Poor Jim. What if he couldn't fix it this time? The news was like a dark blanket thrown over the fears already lurking in my mind.

Oh, God, I feel so awful. How are we going to make it? I wanted to crawl in bed, pull the covers over my head, and sleep forever.

With darkness approaching, I pulled on the overhead bulb dangling from the ceiling. I was about to draw the shades, closing us in for another night in our fight for survival, when I caught sight of Mrs. B. at the back door. *What does she want now?*

Within moments she stood in the middle of the kitchen floor and lifted a white cloth doily to reveal a pan of buttery brown biscuits whose crusts snuggled together in neat little rows, fragrant, freshly baked.

I had a habit of crying when I felt down and someone was nice to me, and I felt my mouth begin to quiver. I swallowed, thanked her, and glanced aside so as not to let her see the tears coming from the sob crowding my throat.

"Honey," she said in her ringing voice, "the pleasure was all mine. You see, I got to watch those biscuits rise." Then she let out a laugh that came from down deep and crinkled her eyes. "And you know, some days I feel just like that old blob of dough."

I must have looked at her curiously then, for she explained. "Seeing that little miracle, I think about my Lord shaping me into something worthwhile—just like He does my dough, and I just give myself over to Him."

I pulled a chair from under the kitchen table and Mrs. B. slipped off her coat and reached for my squirming bundle. Mute, I handed it over and watched while she dropped into the chair and cuddled our baby to her bosom.

"Yes, sir-ee," she went on, "if my Lord can take a piece of old flat dough and make golden biscuits out of it, just think what He can do with one of His own beings. I live by Psalm 31:1— 'In Thee, O Lord, do I put my trust'!"

Mrs. B. seemed to have the right touch, for our baby was strangely quiet. When Mrs. B. wasn't cooing and lulling with a rocking movement, she talked on. "Just as I have faith that my buttermilk and baking soda are going to make my biscuits rise, I have the knowledge that Christ is going to lift me up when I'm down."

Mrs. B. down? I'd never thought about such a thing. She was always flitting about, seemingly on top of things—unlike melancholy me.

I placed the fragrant biscuits into the warming oven at the top of the stove, stoked the fire, and sat down in the other kitchen chair to listen to Mrs. B.'s lighthearted chatter.

A short time later when I watched Mrs. B. slip into her coat and let herself out, I knew my spirits were lifting. I fed our daughter and, feeling her body mold itself into mine in slumber, I eased her into the large carriage we used as a bassinet. Then, with a surge of energy I had not felt in a long, long time, I climbed up to the cabinet where we'd stored the blackberry jelly made last summer from berries gathered along a country road.

When Jim came in, the burden of his troubles etching his face, I had freshened up and set the table with cheese slices, applesauce, and blackberry jelly. The light of a candle gave it all the glow of a special occasion. Then I drew Mrs. B.'s beautiful buttermilk biscuits from the warming oven and their aroma filled the room.

With the carriage pulled close and a nudge from my foot to keep it gently rocking, the baby quietly—miraculously—watched the candle's flickering flame.

Seeing Jim's face relax, I knew that the faith that Mrs. B. had passed along to me was contagious. And there in the glow of the candlelight, our little family—father, mother, and child—came into a mellow circle of love with God in the center.

In my anguish I had questioned God's presence, I had poured out my heart in my misery, but I had not, as Mrs. B. said, allowed Him to take over my weary body and mold me into something new.

And since then, whenever I'm depressed, I remember Mrs. B. and her buttermilk biscuits. It reminds me to put my trust in the Lord, because I know He is there and will lift me up.

A Guy Who Went Wrong
by Frank R. Minucci

EVERY YEAR, TWO DAYS BEFORE THANKSGIVING, MY WIFE, PATTY, AND I HAVE A LITTLE CEREMONY—NOTHING FANCY, BUT IMPORTANT TO US. SHE GETS HER JEWELRY BOX, TAKES OUT A STRING OF MEDALS, AND PRESENTS ONE TO ME. THEY'RE THOSE SUNDAY SCHOOL MEDALS WE USED TO GET FOR PERFECT ATTENDANCE. FIRST YOU GOT A WHITE ENAMELED PIN WITH A RED CROSS ON IT. THE NEXT YEAR, A GOLD-PLATED WREATH WAS ADDED. THE THIRD YEAR, AND EVERY YEAR THEREAFTER, YOU GOT A BAR, SUSPENDED FROM THE MEDAL BY TINY GOLD CHAINS.

You're probably wondering what a grown man is doing getting Sunday school medals. Let me tell you how I got them in the first place.

I grew up in a series of foster homes in northern New Jersey, where the foster parents regularly reminded me how lucky I was "to have Johnny share his room with me." One family used to lock me in a dark closet in the cellar.

Then I got lucky. I was sent to live with Mom and Pop Klein. They were strict German Lutherans, good people with a loving but disciplined home.

They sent me to Sunday school. I loved it, especially the flannel-graph stories about Jesus; the teacher used to let us move the figures around. When I was nine I won a trip to Bible camp for memorizing the names of all the books of the Bible. Mom Klein was so proud of me! And I was collecting a long string of those perfect-attendance medals.

But in my teenage years I began to rebel against the Kleins' all-work-and-no-play rules. When I was fifteen I ran away. Besides, I decided, if my real mother and father didn't want me, I didn't want anybody as my parents.

Out on the streets of north New Jersey cities, I embarked on a life of crime. Over the next twenty years, I was into everything—car theft, burglary, "collecting" for loan sharks, and managing underworld "social clubs" with their drugs, gambling, and prostitution. (I spent six years in and out of reform schools, and later a short term in prison for extortion.) I never joined the inner circle; I was what you might call a "middle-management mobster."

But along the way I got a reputation for being a little crazy. Once, as a warning, I literally parted a rival's hair with a double-barreled shotgun. And when I divorced my wife of thirteen years for running around on me, I told her in a real nice way not to bother me about anything—or I'd kill her. And she knew I meant it. (However, I wasn't totally rotten: I did give her support for our four kids.)

After our divorce, I had a short encounter with Christianity. I went forward at a church service some guy dragged me to. I even made a decision for Christ. But I soon fell back into my old ways.

You remember how Jesus said that when you kick a demon out, it goes and gets seven more demons that are even worse, and it comes back? Well, that's what happened to me. The devil greased the old slide and I went backward into another ten years of crime. Now I had nice clothes, a big car, and women. The devil had me in his grip.

Then I met Patty. She was a good Italian girl, raised strict by her grandmother, the kind of girl who listened to Christian radio. *How can she care about a bum like me?* I wondered. Yet she did. She saw something behind the meanness and hate. She just reached inside of me—and I fell in love with her. She made my life so wonderful!

I took Patty to meet Mom Klein. (Pop had passed away.) I liked visiting Mom, but she always lectured me. "Frankie," she'd say in her heavy German accent, "they that live by the sword shall die by the sword." But she loved Patty; Mom was sure Patty would set me straight.

We got married. It was like a Hollywood romance. Patty made everything brand new.

I dropped out of organized crime and tried to go straight. But I couldn't get a decent job. All I knew was crime. We had six kids between us (four of mine, one of hers, and one of ours). I wound up borrowing money from my next-door neighbor to buy milk.

I began to make little marijuana deals on the side. What else was I going to do? Then I discovered cocaine, which was getting to be the "in" drug in the early 1970s. One night at a party at a fancy Manhattan penthouse, I tried some coke, out of curiosity.

Soon I was making lots of money dealing cocaine. I had five guys pushing it on the streets. I bought Patty and the kids everything they needed or wanted: clothes, toys, bikes, cars, furniture. We even owned two big boats.

Patty was worried. She told me it was dirty money and that she was praying for me. "It's puttin' clothes on your back!" I snarled. The tug-of-war between my family life and my drug dealing was beginning to make me feel I was in a closet again, like when I was a kid. It was a big closet, a nice closet, but still a closet.

Then I broke the cardinal rule of coke trafficking: If you deal it, don't do it.

Soon I was doing it all the time. I was doing so much I was diluting the stuff I was supposed to sell. The coke was so bad my customers refused to pay. But I had to pay my suppliers. I began to owe money.

Cocaine addiction makes you paranoid. You think everyone is out to get you. (In my case, a few guys were.) I began carrying a .32-caliber five-shot pistol in my belt and a .38 strapped to my ankle. One night, I heard somebody sneaking around in the dark. I grabbed the guy and held a gun to his head. It was my oldest boy, Ronnie—and I almost killed him. That scared me.

Another night, I was high and said to Patty, "You think I don't love you?" And I took a lighted cigarette and stuck it on my hand and said, "All the pain you can put on me I can take." She started to scream.

I suspect that through all the sickness and perversity I was still a little kid locked in a closet in the cellar and crying, "Why won't they let me out? Why don't nobody love me? Why don't nobody want me?"

Some so-called experts say that coke isn't addictive. They're liars. I had nose polyps and trouble with my bodily functions; I was bleeding. But when I tried to stop, I could hardly breathe.

One night in early November 1984, my little son, Angelo, age three, was fiddling with the dial on my radio. I chased him out. When I turned the radio on, the first word I heard was "cocaine." This baseball player, Darrell Porter, was on a Christian talk show, telling how cocaine wrecked his life, until he found God.

Yeah, I thought, *I tried that God bit too.* I switched to my country-and-western station and did some coke.

A couple of nights later I woke up with sharp pains in my head, like somebody was shoving hatpins into my brain. The pains wouldn't go away. Staring in a mirror, I saw that my face looked like snakeskin.

I shut myself up in my den. I gulped Tylenol, Valium, everything I had, but the pain wouldn't stop. I can take pain—I've been shot and stabbed, but this time it felt like my head was going to explode.

I went and lay down by Patty. A crushing pain tipped across my chest. "I think I'm having a heart attack!" I rasped.

"Just try to breathe normally, Frank. I'll call an ambulance!"

"No! Don't call an ambulance!" But the pain was excruciating. I jumped up and paced around and around the house. Patty was scared, but she wouldn't disobey me.

Now the pain in my chest turned to numbness. I stuck my head in the freezer, trying to suck in the cold air. "I can't breathe," I gasped. "I'm cold." Patty wrapped me in a blanket and rocked me.

There was a bag of cocaine on the table. A voice spoke in my head: "Take another line...just one more line, Frankie. It'll help you." I hunched over the stuff.

"Frank—do you have to do that?" Patty asked, her voice full of fear and despair. Ignoring her, I snorted the whole bag, well over a gram of coke.

I stood and took three steps. A freezing sensation hit my chest, fanning out across both shoulders and down my arms. I tried inhaling, but nothing happened. I grabbed the chair and began falling...falling. Wind seemed to be rushing past me. I started to gag on my tongue.

For some reason, I was thinking about that ballplayer, Darrell Porter, I'd heard on the radio, what he said about drugs and God. I pictured my little Angelo looking at me dead on the floor.

No—no! I cried to myself. *Lord God, please take this from me! If You do, I'll serve You the rest of my life! I'm not asking for myself, God, but don't do this to my kids, don't let 'em have a dead junkie for a father! I promise I'll change!*

Over my head I felt a warm breeze, something like a hair dryer on low. This breeze just came down over me, engulfing me. I smelled the sweetest smell of flowers—roses, violets. The sweet breeze was like honey around my head. My brain cleared, the shooting pains stopped. The honeyed breeze crept down to my chest. My lungs opened and I could breathe again. The sweet, sweet smell of flowers was everywhere—flowers and honey.

Patty was looking at me, amazed. "How—how do you feel?"

"I—I feel pretty good." It was the understatement of my life. I couldn't believe what had just happened to me.

I looked in a mirror. My eyes were clear, my skin was no longer blotchy and bloated. My cheeks were pink.

"Frank," Patty said, "do you realize that God just gave us a...miracle?"

"Naaah!" I said, suddenly scared. "Don't give me that religious business."

"How can you say that? You're going to deny it?"

"We'll see!" I said, going into the bedroom, slamming the door. I went to the closet, rummaged around, and got my Bible down. Holding it up, I cried, "God, I'm only gonna look once. And You'd better show me that it was You who did this. And if You don't show me it was You, then forget it!"

A Voice spoke. Audibly. It surrounded me, strong and clear, but gentle: "My son, Ezekiel thirty-seven, five and six."

I was stunned. The only verse I could remember from Sunday school was John 3:16. Where is Ezekiel? Someplace in the Old Testament. Mentally, I tried running through the books of the Old Testament I had memorized as a boy. It was hopeless. I thumbed through the Bible until I found Ezekiel, then chapter 37, verse 5.

It blew me away.

"Thus saith the Lord God unto these bones; Behold, I will cause breath to enter into you, and ye shall live: And I will lay sinews upon you, and will bring up flesh upon you, and cover you with skin, and put breath in you, and ye shall live; and ye shall know that I am the Lord."

Don't ask me to explain it, but I was totally healed of my drug addiction. Within two weeks I returned to church and recommitted myself to the Lord. Patty also made a decision for Christ. Ditto our kids.

Patty sold her jewelry. I sold my fancy cars. We paid every cent we owed.

Patty and I went back to visit Mom Klein to share the good news with her. I hadn't seen Mom in almost six years. She was now in her eighties and had bone cancer.

She was so happy to see us, but she was puzzled by my Christian talk. "What is this 'Praise the Lord' every two minutes?" she asked.

"I'm just happy about Jesus, Mom," I replied. "Does it bother you?"

"No—not if you mean it."

She knew she was dying. She gave me Pop's old binoculars and the concertina he loved to play. She gave Patty snapshots of me when I was a little boy.

"And now, smart guy," she said to me, "come over here. See this?" And she held up the string of Sunday school medals. "You had a good foundation. Here, wear this!" And she poked a frail finger at my lapel.

"Mom, I can't wear all them medals at once. It's too much!"

"Okay," she says, drawing herself up (all four-feet-eleven of her), "you can earn them all over again. Patty, you make sure. Every year goes by and Frank is still a Christian, he gets one—first the pin, then the wreath, then the bars. All over again, he'll earn them. Promise me." And she pressed them into Patty's hands.

Four months later we prayed Mom home with the Lord.

So now you know why, each November, we'll get Patty's jewelry box and say a little prayer, thanking God for His mercy and forgiveness. Because no man is beyond redemption, if he truly repents.

Then Patty will lovingly pin on my third bar. And I'll imagine Mom up in heaven saying, "Dis iss goodt, Frankie!"

10.

A Reason for Hope
by Jim Hinch

I WAS RIDING IN THE BACKSEAT OF AN SUV WHEN I FIRST SAW NEW ORLEANS. IT WAS A GAUZY, MUGGY MORNING, THREE DAYS AFTER HURRICANE KATRINA HIT. THE STORM HAD REDUCED THIS MOST MYTHICAL OF AMERICAN CITIES TO A VISION OF THE APOCALYPSE. A PHOTOGRAPHER AND I WERE DRIVING OVER THE MISSISSIPPI RIVER WITH THE WORDS OF A POLICE OFFICER AT A CHECKPOINT STILL BUZZING IN OUR EARS, "IF YOU GO THERE, YOU'LL PROBABLY BE KILLED." WE PULLED TO THE SIDE OF THE BRIDGE AND LOOKED OVER THE RAILING. THE CITY, DROWNED IN STILL, BLACK WATER, REFLECTED THE SKY AND THE RISING SUN IN A LATTICE OF SUBMERGED STREETS. A FUNNEL OF SMOKE FROM A CHEMICAL WAREHOUSE FIRE TRAILED TO THE HORIZON. *GOD HAS LEFT THIS PLACE*, I THOUGHT.

Twenty-four hours earlier I had been sitting at my desk in New York, where I worked as a newspaper reporter. My phone rang. "Can you be on a plane to Louisiana this afternoon?" my editor asked. Yes, I said. Then I put the phone down and stared at the wall. What had I just done?

I went home to pack and say good-bye to my wife, Kate. We had just moved to New York in July from California, and married only two months before that. Our life together was just beginning, mine as a reporter for a New York daily and hers as a priest at an Episcopal church. Was I about to jeopardize our future by plunging into a disaster zone? Most of my career as a journalist consisted of calling people and cajoling them into giving me tidbits of information. As I sat in my seat on the plane to Baton Rouge, I could do nothing more than pray. *Let me get through this, Lord. Show me what to do when I get there. Help me get home safe to Kate.*

I met the photographer, Matt, at the airport and we loaded our rented SUV with food, water, and rubber boots. We took back roads toward the city and used a flashing orange emergency light to get past checkpoints. When we reached the city, we found bodies lying on the sidewalks and, farther on, floating in poisoned water that rose to the roofs. We saw office buildings toppled into chunks of brick and left to burn by a fire department with no running water. And we saw the roaming, desperate survivors clustered along the sides of the highways. By this time they had gone days with no food or water. Babies were dehydrated. Grandparents sat in broken wheelchairs under a pitiless sun.

Matt and I waded into crowds, and people called out to us, even grabbed us. Several cried with relief that someone had come to tell their story. And, strangely enough, that's when my fears left me. From a distance the city had looked moribund, desolate. Now, among the people, we saw that the city was alive. Desperate, but alive. What mattered was finding and telling these people's stories.

I discovered glimmers of dignity and generosity. Picking my way through the urine-soaked, trash-strewn streets in front of the convention center, I met Roynell Joshua, a seventy-two-year-old man who sat with limbs askew in a folding chair on the blistering pavement. He was surrounded by thousands waiting for evacuation buses that had been promised but hadn't arrived. Roynell, who had climbed out a window of his flooded home into a rescue boat, needed dialysis. He had missed three treatments since the storm hit. He was weak almost to the point of incapacity. Each leg was the diameter of a baseball bat. When someone tried to move him, his face seized with pain and he cried out, "No! No! No!"

His situation seemed impossible. But then a woman sitting next to him spoke up, "He fell in the street trying to cross over here. I got some guys to help get him. We've been on this spot for two days. We sit and talk. It keeps me busy."

The woman was Darleen Morgan. She had lost her house and her family. She had never met Roynell, but when she saw him slip in a puddle and fall, she helped him up. Now she sat beside him, shielding him with an umbrella and holding a bottle of water to his lips.

"She's doing a good job," Roynell said.

And there was Brad Mercer, a special-education mediator from a Dallas suburb who drove five hundred miles in a fifty-foot-long amphibious tourist ferry called the Duck to pull the lost and the frail from drowned New Orleans homes. I rode with Brad on his boat through a flooded neighborhood near downtown, and he told me how watching news images after the storm got him increasingly agitated, until he impulsively cleared out his work calendar for a week and drove the Duck with a friend to New Orleans.

Their boat looked like a giant soap dish with wheels. Rescue workers rejoiced at it because it could plunge into streets too shallow for most boats and too deep for trucks. The afternoon I rode the Duck we motored through streets that bobbed with sodden sofas, police cars, and swimming dogs. We reached a school where twenty-five survivors had been stranded for days.

They loaded in, carrying bags that held all they owned. Cornelius Victor, fifty-two, had sloshed his way to the school with his wife and younger brother, Ronnie, who was so horrified by what he had seen in the hurricane's aftermath that he couldn't speak. But Cornelius told me how, each day, he had lathered himself with Vaseline and plunged into the murky waters to take food to elderly neighbors and stranded pets.

For every scene of despair I witnessed in New Orleans, there was a Cornelius Victor. Or a Brad Mercer, who, in his haste to get to New Orleans, drove in shifts with his friend and slept in the metal hull of the Duck. Or a Darleen Morgan. I had witnessed devastation here. But none of my fears were realized. Instead, I found courage and tears where I expected to find violence. I found ragged attempts to preserve dignity where I expected to find the breakdown of civilization. I found faith where bitterness could have taken hold. And I found that in a fallen world where people so often think only of themselves, the horror of disaster can prompt a selflessness we would otherwise never achieve.

And most important, I found a kind of answer to the question formed by disaster: "Where are You, God, in this?" He was everywhere. I could feel His presence with the suffering of His people. Perhaps it sounds perverse to say so, but in New Orleans, where all love seemed lost, I found a deeper love that holds the afflicted close enough to offer them redemption. For God is never closer to us than when we are suffering, and hope is never nearer than when we need it most.

The Distance
by Meb Keflezighi

I WAS ONE OF THE FAVORITES TO WIN THE RACE THAT COOL NOVEMBER DAY IN NEW YORK CITY, THE MARATHON TO QUALIFY FOR THE US OLYMPIC TEAM. I'D WON THE SILVER MEDAL IN ATHENS, AND NOW MY SIGHTS WERE SET ON BEIJING 2008. ALL I NEEDED WAS TO FINISH IN THE TOP THREE HERE. I GOT OFF TO A GOOD START, LOOPING AROUND CENTRAL PARK. I WAS IN THE FRONT OF THE PACK, RIGHT WHERE I WANTED TO BE. I FELT GOOD.

Suddenly there was pain in my calves, followed by a sharp pain in my right hip. Run through it, I tried to convince myself. Ignore the pain. But it got worse. By mile twelve I knew I couldn't win the race. If I kept going, doing the best I could, maybe I could hang on to second place. One runner passed me. Then another. And another. By the end, guys were going by me like I was standing still. I came in eighth. No chance of making the Olympics, even as an alternate. I hobbled away from the finish line. The pain was excruciating.

A friend rushed up to me. His face looked serious, and I assumed he was worried about me. Instead he asked, "Did you hear about Ryan?" Ryan Shay was a good friend, one of my training partners.

He'd been right next to me on the bus ride to the race. I shook my head.

"Ryan collapsed maybe five miles in," he said. "A heart attack. They couldn't do anything for him. He died."

My mind refused to accept it. No, not Ryan. How could Ryan be dead?

He and I had trained together in Mammoth, California, with Running USA, racing through the hot dry summer, the autumn when the aspens shimmered, the winter when we raced over snow. He was one of the strongest, toughest guys I knew. He'd just gotten married. He had so much to live for. And now—

I went to pieces. Tears came so hard I couldn't stop them.

My friend helped me to a taxi and took me back to my hotel. The pain in my hip had grown so bad I had to crawl around my room on my hands and knees. But the emotional anguish of losing my friend, that was even worse.

My wife, Yordanos, tried to comfort me. "Meb, you don't have to keep running. You have a college diploma. There are other things you can do."

True, I had a degree in communications. I could find a job in that field. But I kept thinking of something my father told me when I was growing up, "God has great plans for you." Only God could have brought my family safely from Africa to America, only He could have given me my talent for running. Was I wrong to believe He wanted me to make something more of that gift?

If it hadn't been for the grace of God, I wouldn't have been running for America, or even running at all. I might still be in the farming village where I was born in Eritrea, a small country on the horn of Africa. We lived in a stone hut with no running water, no electricity, no TV, no phone. All my family had were a few cows, donkeys, sheep, and goats. And the six of us children had the faith our parents nurtured in us.

My father had been a freedom fighter in the war against Ethiopia and it wasn't safe for him in Eritrea. When I was five, he had to flee for his life. "How long will it be until we see you again?" my oldest brother asked. My father couldn't answer. He hid his face, not wanting us to see him crying.

After spending two years in Sudan, he settled in Italy and found work. For five years, our only connection were the letters and gifts he sent. Shirts, sweaters, pants, shoes. "I told the salesman how old my children are," my dad wrote. "He thought these would be the proper sizes." The shoes were always too big.

At last Dad saved enough money to send for us, but Italy was only a stop on our journey. Our destination was America, the land of freedom and opportunity, the country of my father's dreams. "It is a beautiful place," he told us. "Everybody can go to school and get an education. You can become whatever you want to be."

I was twelve when we arrived in San Diego, California, on October 21, 1987—a date I will never forget. A new sister had been born in Italy, so we were now a family of nine. We crowded into a small apartment. We walked everywhere, trying to understand this new land of big cars, tall buildings, and fast food. One day my brothers and I went to the park near our apartment to play soccer. We saw dozens of kids running across the grass. A few years later I would find out it was the national high school cross-country championships, but back then it just seemed strange to me. *What are those crazy people running for?* I wondered. *What are they chasing?* There was no ball, like in soccer. Just a trail through the eucalyptus and palms.

What my father told us made much more sense to me. "The only way you'll get ahead is through education," he said. "You must work very hard and get the best grades." An A minus or a B plus would not do. It had to be an A. To make sure we learned English and did our homework, he woke us up at 4:30 in the morning to study. Yes, 4:30. It was the only time he had to help us between his night job cleaning offices and his day job driving a taxi.

"Switch on the light," he said. "Time to study." There was no argument. We sat at the kitchen table and worked until 6:45, then went off to school. "I was not able to stay in school past seventh grade," he told us. "I want you to go further. I want your life to be better than mine. That is every father's dream."

Every week in seventh grade we had races in gym class. One Friday the teacher said, "Today we're going to do the mile. Do your best and I'll give you an A or a B. But if you just mess around, you'll get a D." I had never done a mile, but I knew I had to get an A, so I ran as hard as

I could. I beat all the other boys. The teacher stared at his stopwatch. "You just ran a 5:20 mile—without any training!" he said. He called the high school coach right away and told him, "We've got a future Olympian here."

That had to be part of God's plans. It was something I never would have dreamed myself! I joined the cross-country and track teams. I won races. Senior year, I was one of those kids running at the park in the high school championship. Bob Larsen, the track-and-field and cross-country coach at UCLA, gave me a full scholarship. I won four NCAA titles, but it wasn't just about doing well on the track. I did well in the classroom too. I was proud and grateful to receive my diploma in 1998, as proud and grateful as I was to become a US citizen later that year. I knew my father spoke the truth: in America, my education would take me where I needed to go, even when my legs no longer could.

Yet here I was in a New York City hotel room, nearly a decade after college, grieving the loss of my friend Ryan, nursing my battered body, and wondering what I should do with my life. I'd had an excellent career as an elite distance runner. Had the moment come when my legs could no longer carry me? Was it time to retire? Finally I said to Yordanos, "Let's pray." We took each other's hands and closed our eyes. "God, thank You for the gift of running," I said. "I have tried to do my best with it. If it is time for me to move on, please tell me."

I thought of the many miles I had run with Ryan, stride by stride, seeing the sunlight coming through the trees, the breathtaking mountain views. I loved getting to know a town with each step I ran through its streets and parks and woods. Just thinking of how more of the world opens up when I'm out running filled me with joy—a joy that could only come from God, a joy that I wasn't ready to give up.

I opened my eyes and looked at Yordanos. "I don't think I'm meant to quit," I said. "Not yet. I have to keep trying." I believed that was what God wanted. I knew it was what Ryan would have wanted.

I needed a year of rehab and physical therapy to recover from what turned out to be a stress fracture of my hip. But eventually I was training again on the trails I'd run with Ryan. Eventually I went back to New York for a race that would take me through Central Park, where I'd gotten the terrible news of his death. I was running the New York City Marathon. No American had won since Alberto Salazar in 1982.

This time an American did, a man who was born in a tiny village halfway across the world. A man who did not make his long journey alone. He had a mother and father who taught him the power of faith and education, coaches and teachers who helped him believe in himself, good friends who trained with him, a wife who understood him in a way that went beyond words and, most of all, a God Who had boundless love for him.

That cool November day, I turned into Central Park with two miles to go and pulled away from my closest competitor. On the homestretch, I passed the spot where my friend Ryan fell. I said a prayer and made the sign of the cross. Then I crossed the finish line first.

12.

Digging Deep
by Jerry Ellis

THAT WAS THE LAST PLACE I WANTED TO BE—ABOARD AN AIRPLANE HEADED TO CONNECTICUT FOR A VA REHABILITATION PROGRAM FOR THE BLIND, HUNDREDS OF MILES AWAY FROM MY HOME AND FAMILY. I SHIFTED IN THE SEAT AND FOCUSED ON THE FAINT GLOW I KNEW MUST BE THE SUNLIGHT COMING THROUGH THE WINDOW, WONDERING WHAT HAD HAPPENED TO THE EAGER EIGHTEEN-YEAR-OLD KID I HAD BEEN WHEN I FIRST RODE AN AIRPLANE ON MY WAY TO US MARINE CORPS BOOT CAMP BACK IN 1960. THE WORLD WAS FULL OF POSSIBILITIES THEN; THOSE POSSIBILITIES HAD BECOME AS DARK AND VAGUE AS MY EYESIGHT.

I had grown up in West Virginia hill country, one of twelve kids. No matter how tight money was, Mama made sure we never went hungry—she could fix a tasty meal with just a handful of vegetables and a sprinkle of spices. On chilly, gray days, all it took for me to feel warm again was a good whiff of whatever was bubbling in the cast-iron pot on the stove. She passed on her skills to us kids, and cooking became one of my favorite hobbies, the measuring and mixing of ingredients a way of sorting out what was going on in my life.

Another constant in my childhood was faith. I could always count on someone, usually my aunt Callie May, taking me to our small, crowded church every Sunday. "Trust in the Lord and He'll always take care of you," she said. I stared at the flames in the potbellied coal stove that heated our church, daydreaming about the future God planned for me.

I thought I had found that future when I became a marine. But in 1964, during a routine gas-mask training exercise, one of my lungs ruptured. I was rushed to surgery, but it was too late; doctors couldn't save the lung. For years, I battled one wicked bout of pneumonia after another. Finally, I was medically discharged from the service in 1969.

Coal was pretty much the only industry in my hometown, so—despite my missing lung—I went to work as an electrician in the mines. I married Helen in 1971, and soon we had our kids, Tina and Jerry. Sometimes it got to me that I didn't have the energy to play ball with my son or give my daughter a piggyback ride, but I was proud that I was supporting them. Even when I had trouble breathing way down deep in the mines, I kept going because every day meant money toward a new cheerleading uniform for Tina or a fishing trip with Jerry.

But by the mid-eighties, my remaining lung couldn't take it anymore, and I had to quit working. My family was forced to scrape by on my monthly disability pension from the VA. I fixed things around the house; I helped Helen in the kitchen. At least I was doing something. Then in 1989 came a crushing blow: I developed a brain tumor that left me unable to walk, talk, or eat. An operation restored most of my abilities, but I was left partially paralyzed on my left side, deaf in one ear and, worst of all, legally blind. The world was reduced to vague outlines weaving in and out of my vision like ghosts, taunting me with hints of what I would never again see. I had fought through pain and fatigue for years in the mines to have the means to make my children happy, yet I could no longer gaze at their smiles. Day in and day out, I huddled in bed, shaking off my family's attempts to cheer me up, trying to sleep as much as possible so I didn't have to think about how useless I had become.

One afternoon I lay with my face buried in my pillow. *Why has this happened to me, Lord?* I asked. *I've always tried to do right by my family, by my country, and by You. Why have You left me like this? I trusted in You.*

"Come out with us," my wife coaxed gently. "It's a beautiful day."

"Don't feel like it," I mumbled.

Helen sat down on the bed beside me. "Jerry, listen, you can't go on like this. I really think you should go to that program the doctor told you about. That blind rehabilitation."

The thought of starting over again was just too overwhelming. I didn't even want to get out of bed. Why bother? I couldn't work; I couldn't find my way around the house; I couldn't even get myself a glass of water.

"What good will that do?" I said to Helen. "Three months trying to do all the things I can't do anymore."

"Is that any worse than lying here feeling the way you do now?" she said. "You've got to give this a try."

Eventually I didn't have the energy to argue with her anymore. So here I was, picking at bland airplane food as my mind raced with fears—of getting sick on the plane, of not being met at the airport when I got to Connecticut, of what was in store for me at the program. I felt more afraid than I ever had.

A program instructor met me when I got off the plane, but I was still tense the whole drive to the blind center. *This will just make me feel more worthless*, I told myself. Instead of joining the others in the common area after the orientation that evening, I retreated to my room to call my family.

"I can almost taste that chicken and mashed potatoes you're cooking from here, honey," I said, clasping the receiver tightly with both hands. "Wish I was there." Helen gave me a pep talk, and after we hung up I groped my way to the window and opened it a crack to try to catch a scent of the vegetable garden they had taken us through. I thought of all the places I had been—in the marines I had looked forward to each assignment as a new adventure, but now all I wanted was to go home. I shoved my hand in my pocket and ran a finger along the grooved metal of my house key. If only I could get back to the airport or even to a bus station, I could catch the first ride back. But I was trapped. *Okay, Lord, I'm here, but now what?*

The next morning an instructor got me up, took me out into the center of town, and began teaching me how to cross streets safely and get where I wanted to go. Next, she sent me out on my own. I had to be mighty resourceful to avoid getting stranded. By the end of the week I had begun to feel a little more confident. During group activities I got to know my classmates, some of whom were totally blind and in wheelchairs to boot. *If they can do this, maybe I can too,* I allowed.

Together we practiced basic things like buttoning our clothes correctly and cutting apples, then moved on to buying groceries and setting up systems to simplify finding items in cabinets. *Thank You, God, for my being able to walk out here in the fresh air,* I found myself thinking one day as I tapped down a sidewalk with a red-and-white cane.

One morning I awoke early with the urge to go outside. I made my way to the vegetable garden. I stood for a moment, inhaling the rich, earthy smell that reminded me of Mama's kitchen so long ago. Then I dropped to my knees. I dug my fingers into the soil and felt a turnip stem. A bee buzzed by my ear and the breeze sneaked under my shirt as I yanked the vegetable out of the earth. I brushed the dirt off that plump treasure, set it down, and picked some tomatoes from vines nearby.

I breathed deeply. Peppermint. I crawled toward it and picked some, then caught a whiff of another spice—and another—rosemary, thyme, garlic, dill. Everywhere I turned I smelled yet another aroma from my childhood, and I rushed to touch and taste them all. Each time I harvested a spice, it was as if I were unearthing hope buried deep inside me—another possibility I had thought was lost. *Maybe there's still something out there for me,* I thought. I raised my head and felt the sun on my cheeks. *With Your help, Lord, I know I can find it.*

I fingered the smooth, waxy skin of sweet peppers and brushed crinkly lettuce leaves across my cheek. My stomach growled. *What a salad this would make!* I thought. For the first time since the brain tumor, there was something I really wanted to do. I wanted to cook a mouthwatering meal just like Mama used to.

It took a little convincing, but the program directors let me and two friends make Thanksgiving dinner for the more than forty other program participants. You name it, it was on the menu: roast turkey, dressing, ham, potato salad, green beans, macaroni salad, pineapple upside-down cake. And a salad with vegetables and spices from the garden. The feast went so well, I was offered a job in the kitchen. But I had a vision of my own.

"You know what?" I said to my new friends. "When I get back home, I'm going to open a restaurant. Folks in my neck of the woods are always saying they'd like a place where they can get a good, fast bite to eat."

"You kidding?" one guy said. "Look at all the work tonight took."

"I don't care. I've always loved to cook. And I know this'll go over big."

As I packed my belongings on the last day of the program, I checked for my keys and remembered how I had wished I had been able to get a plane or bus home that first night. Now I felt I could walk all the way home with what I had learned.

At the airport I greeted Helen and told her about my idea in the same breath. The next day, she drove us to the VA Regional Office.

My counselor led me into his office. "You're looking well, Jerry. How can I help you today?"

I poured out my restaurant idea, explaining that my wife would help me with the business side. "Sounds like you got yourself a plan there, Jerry," he said slowly. "We can help you with resources. But, you know," he added, "if you go through with this, you're going to lose your pension. And it's going to be a lot of hard work."

"Hard work never scared me any," I said. Helen and I put together a business plan. Two weeks later we got approval, and in October 1994 we opened The Roadside Sandwich and Pizza Shop. We make more than one hundred different items, and get most of our orders from locals and the coal companies.

"Did you really give up a government pension for all this work?" customers often ask me.

"Sure did," I always say. And I've never felt better about my life. I love to chop greens for my famous chef's salad as I listen to gospel music on the tape player and smell the bread baking. Maybe life's colors have faded, but its flavors are sharper than ever. God was taking care of me all along, leading me to a dream that was buried deep within me like the vegetables in the garden. He provided me with the ingredients for a better life, then left it up to me to see how to make something of them.

13.

Surprise!
by Joseph R. Weikel

"CAN YOU THINK OF ANY REASON WHY YOU WOULD NOT WANT TO ACCEPT THE FREE GIFT OF ETERNAL LIFE OFFERED THROUGH JESUS CHRIST?"

My friend Scott, who worked in my office, sat there smiling. Faintly I could hear the cicadas beginning a chorus. It was mid-June in northern Virginia, and we sat in rattan chairs on his back porch. I smelled chicken cooking in the oven. It was a beautiful summer evening, but I was more depressed than usual. It was my birthday and no one had remembered—not my father, my brother, my kids, and certainly not my estranged wife.

My mind whirled. The cicadas were working themselves into a frenzy. It was hard to concentrate. Intellectually, I understood what Scott wanted me to do, but I thought I was too intelligent for Bible-thumping religion. One thing I knew for sure: I was not happy. My life was like a car running out of road. My wife was divorcing me. My children did not want to see me. My boss had told me to look for another job. Suicide seemed like a viable option, since no one wanted me around. Even my therapist fell asleep during my ramblings from his couch. *I'm not so bad*, I thought. *It's just that I'm not very exciting.*

Scott waited patiently, but I could not get my tongue to move. Perhaps it was the medication my therapist had prescribed, which I took dutifully three times a day, even though the little yellow pills made me feel groggy, fuzzy-headed. Mental exertion was a real effort.

"Dinner!" Scott's wife, Katie, called from the kitchen doorway. Smiling, she wiped her hands on the blue checkered apron she wore over a navy dress. The aroma of chicken was irresistible.

"You really need to make a decision now, before we go inside," Scott insisted. "You've been sitting on the fence for nine months." He was right. The first time I had gone to his house was the previous Thanksgiving. What had impressed me then was the atmosphere of peace pervading his home. His two children played quietly without fighting. Even the dog was calm. What a contrast with my own home, a bedlam of kids and dog chasing one another. Here I could even hear a grandfather clock ticking. It sounded like my own life was ticking away.

Maybe it will make Scott happy if I simply do what he wants, I thought. He had said that eternal life was the free gift of God to those who would accept it. I was a sucker for anything free. How many things had I bought because of a free gift? *If there's one chance in million he's right*, I reasoned, *I'd be a fool not to go for it.*

"Will you pray with me to receive Jesus Christ as your Savior and Lord?" Scott asked softly. I nodded. Out of the corner of my eye, I saw his wife still standing quietly in the doorway. "We'll be just a moment, Katie," Scott said. She beamed as I bowed my head.

"Repeat this prayer after me," he continued, turning to me. "Lord Jesus, I'm a sinner. Thank You for dying on the cross for me and my sins. I receive You as Savior and Lord. Come into my heart and make me the kind of person You want me to be."

Phrase by phrase I repeated his words. Surprisingly, I felt a sense of relief, as if a terrible weight had been lifted from my shoulders. A peace like I had never known before settled over me. The queasiness in my stomach relaxed. Instinctively I knew God was in control of my life and would handle the problems that had overwhelmed me. My depression lifted. I felt as if I were floating as we went inside to eat. Chicken had never tasted so good!

Afterward, as I rose to leave my friends' home, I mentioned that it was my birthday. Katie, still clearing the dishes from the table, almost dropped a serving bowl on the floor. Excited, Scott said I had been born twice—physically and spiritually—on the same day!

As I drove home, I heard the most beautiful choral music coming from the radio. But when I reached down to turn it off, I discovered the radio had never been turned on! It seemed like a miraculous confirmation that I had made the right decision.

Twenty-one years later, each June 13, I still celebrate a double birthday. My conversion was almost a wager with God. I took a chance on Him and He certainly took a chance on me. Though I have experienced sadness, disappointment, even tragedy, serious depression never returned. In fact, my spirits are always lifted as I recall that birthday God remembered in such a special way.

14.

Listening

by Sally-Ann Roberts

I HAVE TO GET UP BEFORE DAWN TO ANCHOR AN EARLY MORNING NEWS SHOW IN NEW ORLEANS. THE SHOW AIRS AT 6:00 AND I NEED TO ARRIVE AT THE STUDIO BY 4:30 TO GET READY. EVEN BEFORE THAT, THOUGH, I DO MY OWN PREPARATION AT HOME. QUIET TIME, I CALL IT. NO ONE ELSE IS UP. THE HOUSE IS STILL. I CLOSE MY EYES AND LISTEN.

It hasn't always been that way. Quiet time is something I stumbled into in my mid-thirties, at a moment a few years ago when I needed God in a way I had never needed Him before. The first inkling of it came when I was visiting my maternal grandmother at her apartment in Akron, Ohio. I was a young mother and Grandma Sally was well into her eighties.

That day, before lunch, I walked into the living room to see Grandma Sally sitting on the couch, her eyes shut. As I stood there wondering if I should disturb her, she opened her eyes. Looking serene and rested, she smiled and said, "Let me fix you a sandwich."

The daughter of a clergyman, Grandma Sally was a woman of great spiritual strength. Her own faith was considerably tested during the Depression, when my grandfather lost his business, and she supported the family by cleaning houses. My mother remembers times when their electricity, water, and gas were shut off and the family gathered around a kerosene lamp at night for light and warmth.

For years, Grandma Sally remained active in the church her father had started. She taught Sunday school and gave Bible lessons to the neighborhood kids, luring them in with fresh-baked cookies. The pastor of the church had attended those sessions when he was a boy. He told me my grandmother bought him a new pair of shoes when she noticed the scuffed hand-me-downs he wore. There was always an element of practicality to her religion.

So what could she possibly be doing sitting on the sofa in the silence of the living room? I didn't know. And because it seemed like such a private thing, I didn't feel right asking.

The kind of prayer that was familiar to me was when you spoke out loud to God. You said everything that was on your mind and asked for His help. That's the way Mom and Dad had prayed when I was a kid.

Dad was an officer in the Air Force, so we had to move a lot. To Arizona, to Iowa, to Alabama. After we had the station wagon loaded up for those trips, we gathered in a circle, holding hands. Then Dad prayed, "Please be with us, Lord, as we travel. Take us safely to our destination. Help us settle in at the new base."

The hardest time came when Dad was assigned to a base in Canada for a year, and Mom and we kids stayed in Akron. Everyone was solemn as we watched Dad pack his duffel bag. Mom tried to cover her sorrow by bustling around the kitchen. I stood at the screen door and watched my thirteen-year-old brother, Butch, play one last game of catch with Dad before he left. Suddenly, Butch dropped the ball and put the mitt to his face, bursting into tears.

That day when we were gathered in the family circle, Mom said the prayer. "Dear Lord," she prayed, "bring Larry back safely to us." At the end of the year's tour of duty he came back safe and sound, our prayers answered. Much later, after I had kids of my own, I realized Mom must have said countless prayers when she was alone at night that difficult year.

It was only when my career suddenly hit a huge pothole in the early 1990s that I discovered a greater depth of prayer. Back then I was the anchor of a morning show called *Early Edition*, on WWL-TV in New Orleans. In the space of a dozen years, I had gone from being a cub reporter on the city-hall beat to being an education reporter to doing some investigative work, and then anchoring my own show.

I was doing well. My boss and mentor at the station, Joe Duke, the news director, made that clear. What also became clear was that the station was undergoing financial challenges. Joe had intimated that our show might be in trouble. Then one morning, he asked me to come into his office.

There was no hint of his usual genial smile. "We're going to have to cancel *Early Edition*," he said. "We have to make cutbacks. I'm sorry."

"I understand," I said, nodding. But I was trying desperately not to cry. If *Early Edition* was no more, it seemed likely that my employment would be terminated too. I left the office and drove home. I went up to the bedroom, pulled the drapes, and closed the door. Only then did I start crying.

How was I going to find another job I loved as much? How would we survive financially? My husband, Willie, had just started his own business and we were dependent on my salary. Finally I got down on my knees and prayed. "Dear Lord, what are we going to do? I'll never find another job as good as this one . . ."

After a while, I was spent. I couldn't say another word. And that's when I did something I had never done while praying. I closed my eyes and listened. In the silence of the late morning, I listened to the Lord. I didn't hear any specific words, but it was as though God said to me, *I am here. You have nothing to fear.* An extraordinary peace came over me.

Whatever that feeling was, I couldn't live without it. For the next few weeks, I made sure I had some time to myself every day. I got up early to pray. First, I told God what was on my mind. Sometimes I wrote the words, as in a letter. But then came the most important part. I closed my eyes—usually for about half an hour—and listened. Invariably I came away feeling refreshed.

The next time Joe Duke called me into his office I was sure he would be giving me a pink slip. I knew that no matter what happened I could depend on God to be with me. But as I listened to Joe talk, I realized he was asking me to anchor another show.

"I thought you were going to fire me," I finally admitted.

"Fire you?" he said. "I'm giving you a promotion!"

Six months later, my grandmother died. I went to Akron for the funeral and afterward helped Mom clean out Grandma Sally's apartment. That's when I discovered a priceless treasure trove she had left behind: journals she had kept for decades.

Sometimes she had written only a few words: "Went to Sally-Ann and Willie's for dinner" or "Fixed lunch for Lucimarian." But page after page, my gaze was drawn to the same phrase. Whatever else Grandma Sally did, every day she made this notation: "Had Quiet Time."

"What was Quiet Time?" I asked.

"That's when your grandmother sat quietly to be with the Lord," Mom said.

Of course. I thought of the day I had seen Grandma sitting in the living room with her eyes closed, the most peaceful expression on her face.

"She couldn't get through a day without it," Mom said.

"I know," I said. Because now, neither can I. Every morning, I start my day by reading a few passages of Scripture, then sitting quietly. And listening.

15.

Doing (Too Much?) for Others

by Janet Holm McHenry

IT WAS BIRTHDAY NUMBER FORTY-TWO, BUT I'D SWORN OFF CEL-EBRATIONS. I SAVED THEM FOR MY FOUR CHILDREN. MY DAUGH-TER REBEKAH WAS ALREADY IN HER TEENS! THAT, PLUS THE TOUCHES OF GRAY IN MY HAIR, WERE REMINDERS ENOUGH I WAS GETTING OLDER. I DIDN'T NEED CAKE AND CANDLES TO MARK THE OCCASION.

So my day had unfolded as usual. After teaching and working late in my elementary school classroom, I had sat through a college night course. Nobody could say I'd slowed down any, but I sure was beat when I pulled into the driveway.

The ringing phone greeted me. I answered it, dumping my books on top of the mess on the kitchen counter. It was Rebekah's science teacher. Rebekah had missed her second fund-raising meeting—and had been disqualified from the field trip.

I felt queasy. This wasn't just any field trip. Only the top ten stu-dents from the entire school had been picked to go on a three-day excursion to the San Francisco area. To qualify, Rebekah had taken a difficult written and oral exam. She had gotten the best overall score. I'd never been more proud of her.

The field trip was the first academically related thing Rebekah had worked for. Because she was bright and learning came easily, she didn't put much effort into her studies. I worried about how she was going to get ahead. When Rebekah applied herself, she was a straight-A student. But friends had always come first for my big-hearted daughter. When someone needed her help, she dropped everything, studying included. That's why those As appeared only occasionally. With my constant nagging, she seemed to be turning around, making straight As two quarters in a row. I thought I was winning the battle when she earned a place on the trip.

Rebekah breezed by as I hung up the phone. I dove right in. "I thought this year was going to be about learning responsibility," I lectured. "Getting organized. Not forgetting things. Priorities. Why didn't you go to that meeting?"

"I had to...do something for someone," she mumbled.

"And what about you, young lady?" I shot back. "When are you going to do something for yourself, for your education, your future?"

She looked at me like I was speaking another language. *Dear God, she's got to change. For her own good.* Frustrated, I stormed up to bed.

I lay there, staring at the ceiling. I had studied hard all my life, constantly trying to better myself, to improve my mind. I was still taking courses, for goodness' sake, and here was Rebekah, copping out in the eighth grade!

Eighth grade seemed like a million years ago to me. A million and one, I thought wearily, remembering what day it was.

I was on the edge of sleep when my husband opened the door and peeked in. "Janet," he said quietly, "you need to come downstairs."

"I'm tired, Craig. Will you do something about dinner for the kids? It's been a long day. And did Rebekah tell you—"

"Yes, I know about Rebekah. And dinner's been taken care of. But please come down."

The urgency in his voice moved me from the bed down our winding staircase. What was going on? The bottom floor was pitch-black except for a glow from the kitchen. As I turned the last corner on the stairs, I saw the lit candles on a birthday cake. There was more: a clean kitchen, dinner on the table, presents around the cake. Moving closer, I saw that it was shaped like a T-shirt, with "The Best Mom on Earth" unevenly iced across its middle. Forty-two tiny flames vied for space around the message. Rebekah was standing behind the counter, tears dripping down her cheeks as fast as the wax from the skinny candles atop the cake.

"You missed your meeting because of me?"

She nodded, wiping her eyes. I went over and hugged her close. "I'm sorry," I whispered.

After dinner, cake, and presents, Rebekah and I had a long talk. I had never considered what it was like to be on the receiving end of her generosity. "Your friends are blessed, Rebekah. I see that now. But you worked so hard for that trip . . ." I still could not quite fathom why she had given it up.

"You're worth it, Mom," she said with teenage nonchalance, but her big, warm eyes told me she meant it.

"I guess I should lighten up a bit, shouldn't I?" I asked her to forgive me for setting unreasonable standards. It was something I did to myself too.

Rebekah is now a young adult, making excellent grades in college, studying to be a teacher. In my opinion she still overextends herself sometimes, but I am learning to let her be herself. For her own good, and for all the people she touches with her good—and generous—heart.

Someone I Had to Forgive

by Tom Bowers

MY SISTER MARGIE WAS SPECIAL. WE HAD GROWN UP TOGETHER IN LIBERIA, WHERE MOTHER AND DAD WERE MISSIONARIES. TOGETHER MARGIE AND I TOOK TREKS INTO THE JUNGLE, PLAYED GAMES, STUDIED, AND SHARED OUR PLANS AND DREAMS FOR THE FUTURE. I WAS SENT BACK TO THE UNITED STATES TO ATTEND BOARDING SCHOOL IN NORTH CAROLINA; MARGIE JOINED ME THREE YEARS LATER. NEXT TO MY WIFE, CATHIE, MARGIE WAS MY BEST FRIEND. THAT'S WHY IT WAS INCONCEIVABLE TO ME WHEN ON APRIL 29, 1977, MARGIE, TWENTY-FIVE, WAS BRUTALLY MURDERED IN HER OWN APARTMENT IN OAK PARK, ILLINOIS.

I was twenty-seven at the time, living close by in Wheaton with Cathie and our baby boy, Jamie. I had talked to Margie earlier in the evening, as I did almost every evening; she was excited about her job, and I was going to help her move into a new apartment the next day. Only hours later the police called. That call changed my life—twisted it into a knot—for the next fifteen years.

Returning from an errand, Margie was confronted by Thomas Vanda, a young man who demanded to know the whereabouts of

Margie's former roommate and classmate, Esther. Margie refused to tell him. In a rage, Vanda attacked Margie with a hunting knife, stabbing her repeatedly. A neighbor who heard her dying screams telephoned the police, and Vanda was apprehended.

Margie's death was too overwhelming for me to comprehend—let alone accept—all at once. During the days and weeks that followed I tried to come to grips with her murder. Time and again my thoughts returned to the man who had killed her.

Thomas Vanda had grown up in a middle-class family. In 1971, as a teenager, he had stabbed a girl to death. Initially confined to a mental hospital, Vanda was released in 1976 and sent by social-service agencies to Oak Park. He had occasionally dropped by the neighborhood Bible study Margie and Esther attended.

One year after the murder, I sat in a courtroom. As the trial unfolded, I felt a burning anger. The prosecutor presented the horrific details of that April night. Vanda expressed no remorse. None. As I sat directly behind the smirking killer, it crossed my mind more than once that I could reach across the railing and strangle him.

The jury returned a guilty verdict. Vanda was sentenced to three hundred to five hundred years in the state penitentiary. Justice had been done. "Maybe now I can get on with my life," I told Cathie.

I threw myself into my job as a sales manager. No matter how hard I worked, though, memories of Margie haunted me. I thought of how she had loved to play her guitar and sing. I thought of how much Jamie would have adored his aunt Margie.

More and more, my anger consumed me. My feelings about the loss of my sister, and about the man who took her life, were so strong I sometimes felt physically ill. Usually I was easygoing and took most difficulties in stride. Yet long after the first anniversary of Margie's death, I continued to have moments when the tragedy felt unbearable, and my anger unendurable.

Years passed. My parents, who had returned from Liberia, retired to South Carolina. They too had been profoundly wounded by my sister's senseless death. But they slowly seemed to find closure. "Doesn't it make you sick to know that he's still alive while Margie's gone?" I asked my father.

He only shook his head: "There is evil in this world I can't comprehend. I'd rather try to understand the love of God."

I had fantasies of the night of Margie's murder. I imagined I was present, wresting the knife from Vanda's hand and turning it back on him. The man was a monster; he deserved to die. Running constantly through my thoughts was a desire for vengeance. I would never forgive Thomas Vanda. In a strange way, refusing to forgive became the only revenge available to me.

In 1983 I moved to North Carolina, not far from my parents. For a while my new job distracted me. Inevitably, though, something reminded me of Margie—a dramatic sunset or a lovely solo at church. Even the world's beauty was tainted by my tightly held anger at her killer.

In 1987 I went to a reunion at the boarding school Margie and I had attended in Asheville, North Carolina. I looked across the auditorium and saw a woman with dark-blonde hair coming toward me. It was Margie's former roommate, Esther. As we brought each other up to date on our lives, it was clear Esther had something on her mind. "My life is good," she said. "But I keep searching for some sense of…inner peace. I've done all sorts of things to try to put my mind at rest. Nothing works . . ."

So I was not the only one in the grip of the past. She was the one Vanda had come looking for, and she still felt responsible for Margie's death. She hadn't forgiven herself.

I gently took her by the shoulders. "Esther," I said. "It wasn't your fault. Margie may not be here to forgive you, but I am. I forgive you on her behalf."

Months later Esther wrote me, telling me how my words had released her from her turmoil. She told me that even though the process had taken years, I had "given her wings" to go on with her life.

Wings? I wasn't sure what she meant, but I was happy for her. I didn't think too much about it, though, until I was on my way home from a business trip in West Virginia. I often prepared for the adult Sunday school I taught by listening to tapes on my upcoming lesson topic. As I drove south on Interstate 77, I put a cassette into the tape deck, pushed the play button—and was startled to be reminded of that Sunday's topic: forgiveness.

The speaker read from Matthew 18, Jesus' parable about how we should forgive others seventy times seven. I thought again about my meeting with Esther. *I can tell my class what happened.* I was mentally rehearsing the story as I drove under the high overpass of the Blue Ridge Parkway and descended a steep mountain into North Carolina. Without warning, a storm struck. Rain poured, and thunder echoed across the valley. In that moment, out of nowhere, these words came clearly and astonishingly to my mind: *So you plan to teach about forgiveness? When are you going to forgive?*

Words that direct and powerful had never entered my mind before. The voice had been so real it challenged what had become an underlying assumption of my life: I could never forgive Thomas Vanda. Yet I realized I had been making a choice not to forgive, a choice that was poisoning my life. I could go on hating my sister's murderer, or I could follow Christ's commandment and forgive, a conscious decision that would set me on a different path. But forgive a monster?

In my class that following Sunday, I never mentioned Margie or Esther. Instead, I used platitudes and generalities to talk about forgiveness. At the end of class a woman named JoAnn stopped at the door and turned. "All this stuff you're saying about forgiveness sounds so pat and easy," she said. "But what if somebody harmed your daughter or wife or sister? What would you do?"

In a daze, I went into the sanctuary. At the close of the service I found myself going forward for the altar call. My wife and son followed. Cathie held my hand and Jamie knelt beside us. "Lord," I prayed, "I do not know how to forgive my sister's murderer. Please show me what to do."

Nothing changed suddenly, but changes did come. One day my father prayed with me, then clasped my hands. I found myself doing what I thought impossible—praying for Thomas Vanda. Words I could not escape formed in my mind, as clearly as they had that moment when I was driving along the Blue Ridge Mountains: *It's time. Just forgive.*

Margie would not have wanted my torment to continue. God did not want it. In obedience to God, as well as for my own sake, I had to forgive. At last, I said the words out loud and with conviction: "Thomas Vanda, I forgive you." I said them again and again. "Thomas Vanda,

I forgive you." As I declared my forgiveness, a crushing burden lifted from me and I was filled with a transcendent peace. I finally understood Esther's words: I had been given wings.

We are told to forgive, seventy times seven if necessary. Even then, sometimes it's not enough. Forgiveness is a process, often a long and difficult struggle. Yet in forgiving, we obey God and grow closer to Him, so that eventually His path becomes our path, and even our greatest tragedies become our greatest lessons.

17.

The Jagged Memory
by Lisa Wells Isenhower

WHAT A ROTTEN WAY TO SPEND AN ANNIVERSARY, I THOUGHT,
STARING AT THE BROKEN BATHROOM WINDOW. BURGLARS HAD
USED THE WINDOW ONLY HOURS BEFORE TO BREAK INTO OUR
HOUSE AND ROB US OF OUR TELEVISION AND VCR. I HAD AL-
READY TALKED TO THE POLICE AND THE INSURANCE COMPANY.
NOW I WOULD HAVE TO SWEEP UP THE BROKEN GLASS WHILE I
WAITED FOR MY HUSBAND TO GET HOME FROM WORK.

I stared down at the jagged edges of broken windowpane. An-
niversaries were never easy for me, it seemed. For the second time
today something had robbed me of any feelings of celebration. Earlier, after Bob had given me eight red roses, one for each year we had
been married, three-year-old Andrew asked, "What are those flowers
for, Mama?"

"For Mama and Papa's anniversary," I replied.

"How long have you been married?" asked Rob, who was seven.

"Eight years," I answered as matter-of-factly as I could. But I wondered when Rob's arithmetic would enable him to figure out that his
father and I got married only six and a half months before he was born.

Once, I confided to a friend that I had been pregnant when Bob and I married. She gave me a half-amused, half-puzzled smile and said, "That happens to lots of people! It's no big deal."

But it was a big deal to me. I had gone against the Bible's teaching. I had gone against my own expectations of myself, and I felt ashamed. I bent down and picked up the largest pieces of glass, dropping them into the blue bathroom wastebasket.

Why did this have to happen on our anniversary? I wondered. But I also wondered how I would ever resolve the guilt that was still a part of each anniversary.

I taped an old brochure over the hole in the window to keep the cold and rain out until Bob could replace the pane. He'd promised to take care of it right away.

When Bob arrived home that evening, he wrapped his arms around me and held me a little tighter and a little longer than usual. "Are you okay?" he asked.

"Yes," I replied, then, pulling away, "well…I'm not sure."

"The insurance will cover most of the loss," he began.

"No, it's not that," I said quickly.

"Is it the anniversary? Honey, I'm sorry," he said. "Maybe we can celebrate it on the weekend."

"I don't feel much like celebrating anyway," I replied.

He gave me a questioning look. Unable to explain the strange tangle of emotions I felt, I changed the subject. "Come and see about the window," I said, anxious to get it fixed.

After a brief inspection, Bob assured me he could fix the window. "But it'll have to wait until tomorrow," he said. "The glass place is closed by now."

I scowled at the face on the brochure that covered the broken pane. I had hoped Bob could repair it right away.

We spent a quiet evening at home with Rob and Andrew, trying to explain the robbery to them and assuage their fears that the burglars might return.

Later that night when Bob and I collapsed into bed, I couldn't get to sleep. I listened uneasily to what were surely the usual night noises, wondering where "our" burglars were at that moment.

I glanced over at Bob. His dark head lay motionless on the flowered pillowcase, and I envied his ability to fall asleep so quickly.

I envied too the way Bob had put the past behind him. Why was it so hard for me to forgive myself? Bob and I were still as much in love as ever. We adored our children and taught them to love God as we did. Yet each time our anniversary rolled around, a great sense of disappointment boiled up to obscure my joy.

Daybreak came after a restless night. In the gray light of early morning, I stumbled into the bathroom.

The masking-taped brochure glared at me, reminding me of the previous day's burglary and the night's troubled thoughts. I stood in front of the mirror as I waited for the water in the shower to run hot, vaguely aware of a subtle difference in the room.

It was colder with the hole in the window, yes, but there was something more. As I leaned on the counter to look at my reflection in the mirror, I realized what that difference was.

Through the broken window, I heard birds singing, piercing the dawn silence with their raucous morning song. I turned off the water in the shower and listened for a moment, goose bumps rising on my arms as I heard the world waking.

I thought of all the days I had stood in that same spot inside my bathroom at the same time of morning and had heard nothing. Now, because of a broken window, I was able to witness this early morning concert that had taken place without my notice for so long.

The parallel was immediately apparent. My first pregnancy had been like a broken window that I had tried to cover up, a broken place I wanted to keep hidden. Yet the more I tried to hide my past, the more cut off I became from the beautiful music that God had for me.

"Forgive yourself," God seemed to say. "Accept your broken places, and I will pour through them the music of healing and deep joy."

Suddenly, I felt a new closeness to God. I knew then the truth of the scriptural passage, "The sacrifices of God are a broken spirit; a broken and contrite heart, O God, you will not despise" (Psalm 51:17 NIV). Through a broken window, I had been called back to God's loving embrace.

18.

Unexpected House Call
by Lynne M. Heinzmann

I WAS PACKING UP TO LEAVE THE ARCHITECTURAL FIRM WHERE I'D BEEN WORKING. INTO A BOX WENT MY TEMPLATES, TRIANGLES, AND SCALES, WITH THE PICTURE OF MY DAUGHTERS, JULIA, THREE, AND LAURA, A NEWBORN, ON TOP. *THIS WILL BE A REAL CHANGE FOR ME*, I THOUGHT. NOW I'D BE HOME FULL-TIME WITH LAURA AND JULIA.

My husband, Chris, was also an architect and we worked at the same firm. When Julia was born, Chris and I were able to work out a schedule so that one of us was always home with our daughter. When Laura came along, I expected our routine to continue as before. However, the firm had other plans. My bosses said if I wanted to stay I had to work full-time. So now, sadly, I was leaving.

Chris and I talked for hours, trying to figure out how to handle our budget on his earnings alone. Money would be tight. Before Laura was born we had bought a fixer-upper. Now we'd have no money for any of the renovations. The mortgage payments would be a stretch. And I would have to tell Julia we couldn't go to the movies or buy new toys.

As our lifestyle changed, I found myself feeling uneasy about the future. I couldn't help wondering how we'd make ends meet.

After lunch one afternoon, I promised Julia we'd bake chocolate chip cookies, one of our favorite inexpensive pastimes. Julia helped me mix the batter and spoon out the dough. I slid the cookie sheet into the oven. But when I opened the door to check on them later, the cookies weren't done. I turned the oven on and off. I checked the pilot light. It was lit, but the oven wouldn't fire up. My heart sank. Now there'd be no more baking until we could squeeze money for repairs out of our budget.

The next day, when we were watching one of Julia's favorite videos, the screen went blank. Sound came out, but there wasn't any picture. "Now the TV?" I almost wailed.

Julia's big eyes stared at me. "It's okay, Mommy."

When Chris came home we fiddled with the TV for a long time to no avail. A repairman was out of the question. We'd have to do without.

The next day at lunch I complained about the whole situation as Julia ate a peanut butter sandwich and Laura napped. "I'm not sure how this new arrangement is going to turn out," I said out loud. "And now all these things are going wrong. What are we going to do?"

Julia said, "Mommy, why don't we pray about it?"

"What?" I asked, flabbergasted. I hadn't realized she was listening.

"Why don't we ask God to fix things?" she said. "He can do anything you ask Him to do."

Chris and I had taught Julia that God listens to our prayers and answers them. *I wish it were that simple*, I thought. But if my three-year-old wanted to pray, how could I say no? So we bowed our heads and held hands right at the kitchen table. "Lord, our TV is broken and so is our oven. Please help us get things working again," I said. "And please take care of us in our new situation."

As I started to wash dishes, Julia skipped around the kitchen. "Let's make cookies now," she said.

"But, honey, you know the oven is broken," I said.

"No, it's not," she insisted. "God fixed it. Remember?"

"God will help us in His own time and way," I tried to explain. Then I went over to the oven and turned the dial. "See, it's still broken." I opened the door, but to my utter surprise, the oven fired up right away. "I can't believe it!" I exclaimed. Julia just shrugged her shoulders and smiled.

I walked over to the television and flicked it on. Once again, sound came, but no picture. It was then I noticed one of the adjustment knobs wasn't in its usual position. I was sure that I had turned that knob before. *Might as well try it again*, I thought. A quick twist and the picture came on, clear as day! Just as clear was the message now conveyed to me by a loving God: *Your future is in My hands. Trust Me. Even when times are hard, I'll help you get through them.*

A minute later, Julia and I were in the kitchen mixing batter as the oven heated up. I watched my daughter struggle with the mixing spoon, stirring the eggs and butter and sugar and flour. As I stroked her hair, I felt more relaxed than I had in weeks. *Sometimes*, I thought, *your mommy needs a reminder about who's in charge of our daily lives. Thank you for showing me the power of a simple prayer. And the reassurance of knowing that God does make house calls.*

19.

Where Healing Begins
by Bud Welch

THE FLOOR SHOOK BENEATH MY FEET. I RAN TO THE KITCHEN WINDOW. BLUE SKY, SPRING SUNSHINE. JUST A PEACEFUL OKLAHOMA DAY. IT WAS HARD TO IMAGINE ANYTHING TERRIBLE HAPPENING ON A BRIGHT WEDNESDAY LIKE THAT. I HADN'T PUT ON MY TEXACO UNIFORM THAT MORNING; I WAS MEETING MY TWENTY-THREE-YEAR-OLD DAUGHTER, JULIE, FOR LUNCH. PROUD OF HER? EVERYONE WHO CAME IN FOR AN OIL CHANGE HEARD WHAT A GREAT KID I HAD. SHE'D CAUGHT ME BRAGGING ON HER JUST TWO DAYS BEFORE. "DAD! PEOPLE DON'T WANT TO HEAR ALL THAT!"

Odd, that visit—Julie often stopped by my service station for a few minutes on her way home from her job at the Murrah Building in downtown Oklahoma City (her mother and I were divorced). Monday, though, it was as if she didn't want to leave. She stayed two hours, then threw her arms around me. Julie always gave me a hug when she left, but Monday she held me a long time.

"Good-bye, Daddy," she'd said.

That was odd too. Nowadays Julie only called me Daddy when she had something really important to say. Well, maybe she'd tell me about it that afternoon. Every Wednesday I met Julie for lunch at the Athenian restaurant across from the Murrah Building.

At nine o'clock I'd sat down with that cup of coffee to wait for her call. Julie usually got to work at the Social Security office where she was a translator at 8:00 AM sharp. It was her first job after college. As a federal employee, Julie got only thirty minutes for lunch—and she wouldn't take thirty-one! She always called to find out what I wanted for lunch, then phoned our order in to the Athenian so we could eat as soon as we arrived.

Chicken sandwich this time, I'd decided. The parking lot would be full by lunchtime; I'd see Julie's red Pontiac in her favorite spot beneath a huge old American elm tree. I'd park my truck at one of the meters on the street and watch for her to come out of the big glass doors—such a little person, just five feet tall ("Five feet one-half inch, Dad!"), 103 pounds.

But a big heart. I believed in loving your neighbor and all the rest I heard in church on Sundays. But Julie! She lived her faith all day, every day. Spent her free time helping the needy, taught Sunday school, volunteered for Habitat for Humanity—I kidded her she was trying to save the whole world single-handed.

The rumbling subsided. Bewildered, I stood staring out the kitchen window. Then the phone rang. I grabbed it.

"Julie?"

It was my brother Frank, calling from his car on his way out to the family farm where we'd grown up. "Is your TV on, Bud? Radio says there's been an explosion downtown."

Downtown? Eight miles away? What kind of explosion could rock my table way out here! On the local news channel I saw an aerial view of downtown from the traffic helicopter. Through clouds of smoke and dust, the camera zoomed in on a nine-story building with its entire front half missing. An announcer's voice:

"…the Alfred P. Murrah Federal Building—"

Floors thrusting straight out into space. Tangled wreckage in rooms with no outer wall. And in place of those big glass doors, a mountain of rubble three stories high.

I didn't move. I scarcely breathed. My world stopped at that moment. They were appealing for people not to come into the downtown area, but nothing could have pulled me away from the telephone any-way. Julie would be calling. Her office was at the back of the building, the part still standing. Julie would find her way to a phone and dial my number.

All that day, all that night, all the next day and the next night, I sat by the phone, while relatives and friends fanned out to every hospital. Twice the phone rang with the news that Julie's name was on a sur-vivor's list! Twice it rang again with a correction: The lists were not of survivors, but simply of people who worked in the building.

Friday morning, two days after the explosion, I gave up my sleepless vigil and drove downtown. Because I had a family member still missing, police let me through the barricade. Cranes, search dogs, and an army of rescue workers toiled among hills of rubble, one of them a mound of debris that had been the Athenian restaurant. Mangled automobiles, Julie's red Pontiac among them, surrounded a scorched and broken elm tree, its new spring leaves stripped away like so many bright lives.

Julie, where are you? Rescuers confirmed that everyone else working in that rear office had made it out alive. The woman at the desk next to Julie's had come away with only a cut on her arm. But, at exactly nine o'clock, Julie had left her desk and walked to the recep-tion room up front, to escort her first two clients back to her office.

They found the three bodies Saturday morning in the corridor, a few feet from safety.

From the moment I learned it was a bomb—a premeditated act of murder—that had killed Julie and 167 others, from babies in their cribs to old folks applying for their pensions, I survived on hate. When Timothy McVeigh and Terry Nichols were arrested, I seethed at the idea of a trial. Why should those monsters live another day?

Other memories blur together: Julie's college friends coming from all over the country to her funeral. Victims' families meeting. Laying flowers on my daughter's grave. No time frame for any of it. For me, time was stuck at 9:02 AM, April 19, 1995.

One small event did stand out among the meaningless days. One night—two months after the bombing? Four?—I was watching a TV update on the investigation, fuming at the delays, when the screen showed a stocky, gray-haired man stooped over a flower bed.

"Cameramen in Buffalo today," a reporter said, "caught a rare shot of Timothy McVeigh's father in his—"

I sprang at the set. I didn't want to see this man, didn't want to know anything about him. But before I could switch it off, the man looked up, straight at the camera. It was only a glimpse of his face, but in that instant I saw a depth of pain like—

Like mine.

Oh, dear God, I thought, *this man has lost a child too.*

That was all, a momentary flash of recognition. And yet that face, that pain, kept coming back to me as the months dragged on, my own pain unchanged, unending.

January 1996 arrived, a new year on the calendar, but not for me. I stood at the cyclone fence around the cleared site of the Murrah Building, as I had so often in the previous nine months. The fence held small remembrances: a teddy bear, a photograph, a flower.

My eyes traveled past the mementos to the shattered elm tree where Julie had always parked. The tree was bare on that January day, but in my mind I saw it as it had looked the summer after the bombing. Incredibly, impossibly, those stripped and broken branches had thrust out new leaves.

The thought that came to me then seemed to have nothing to do with new life. It was the sudden, certain knowledge that McVeigh's execution would not end my pain. The pain was there to stay. The only question was what I let it do to me.

Julie, you wouldn't know me now! Angry and bitter, hate cutting me off from Julie's way of love, from Julie herself. There in front of me, inside that cyclone fence, was what blind hate had brought about. The bombing on the anniversary of the Branch Davidian deaths in Waco, Texas, was supposed to avenge what McVeigh's obsessed mind believed was a government wrong. I knew something about obsession now, knew what brooding on a wrong can do to your heart.

I looked again at the tenacious old elm that had survived the worst that hate could do. And I knew that in a world where wrongs are committed every day, I could do one small thing, make one individual decision, to stop the cycle.

Many people didn't understand when I quit publicly agitating for McVeigh's execution. A reporter, interviewing victims' families on the first anniversary of the bombing, heard about my change of heart and mentioned it in a story that went out on the wire services. I began to get invitations to speak to various groups. One invitation, in the fall of 1998, three years after the bombing, came from a nun in Buffalo. Buffalo—what had I heard about that place? Then I remembered. Tim McVeigh's father.

Reach out. To the father of Julie's killer? Not to this guy. That was asking too much. Maybe Julie could have, but not me.

Except Julie couldn't reach out now.

The nun sounded startled when I asked if there was some way I could meet Mr. McVeigh. But she called back to say she'd contacted his church: He would meet me at his home Saturday morning, September 5.

That is how I found myself ringing the doorbell of a small yellow frame house in upstate New York. It seemed a long wait before the door opened and the man whose face had haunted me for three years looked out.

"Mr. McVeigh?" I asked. "I'm Bud Welch."

"Let me get my shoes on," he said.

He disappeared, and I realized I was shaking. What was I doing here? What could we talk about? The man emerged with his shoes on and we stood there awkwardly.

"I hear you have a garden," I said finally. "I grew up on a farm."

We walked to the back of the house, where neat rows of tomatoes and corn showed a caring hand. For half an hour we talked weeds and mulch—we were Bud and Bill now—then he took me inside and we sat at the kitchen table, drinking ginger ale. Family photos covered a wall. He pointed out pictures of his older daughter, her husband, his baby granddaughter. He saw me staring at a photo of a good-looking boy in suit jacket and tie. "Tim's high school graduation," he said simply.

"Gosh," I exclaimed, "what a handsome kid!"

The words were out before I could stop them. Any more than Bill could stop the tears that filled his eyes.

His younger daughter, Jennifer, twenty-four years old, came in, hair damp from the shower. Julie never got to be twenty-four, but I knew right away the two would have hit it off. Jennifer had just started her first job teaching at an elementary school. Some of the parents, she said, had threatened to take their kids out when they saw her last name.

Bill talked about his job on the night shift at a General Motors plant. Just my age, he'd been there thirty-six years. We were two blue-collar joes, trying to do right by our kids. I stayed nearly two hours, and when I got up to leave Jennifer hugged me like Julie always had. We held each other tight, both of us crying. I don't know about Jennifer, but I was thinking that I'd gone to church all my life and had never felt as close to God as I did at that moment.

"We're in this together," I told Jennifer and her dad, "for the rest of our lives. We can't change the past, but we have a choice about the future."

Bill and I keep in touch by telephone, two guys doing our best. What that best will be, neither of us knows, but that broken elm tree gives me a hint. They were going to bulldoze it when they cleared away the debris, but I spearheaded a drive to save the tree, and now it will be part of a memorial to the bomb victims. It may still die, damaged as it is. But we've harvested enough seeds and shoots from it that new life can one day take its place. Like the seed of caring Julie left behind, one person reaching out to another. It's a seed that can be planted wherever a cycle of hate leaves an open wound in God's world.

20.

Day by Day
by Roberta L. Messner

TWO O'CLOCK IN THE MORNING—I WOKE UP WITH NAUSEA AND A SEARING HEADACHE, AS IF A HAMMER WERE BANGING AGAINST MY EYE SOCKETS AND TEMPLES. MY STOMACH CONVULSED. AS I WATCHED THE LUMINOUS NUMBERS ON MY BEDSIDE CLOCK FLIP OVER, SEEMINGLY IN SLOW MOTION, I ASKED MYSELF HOW I COULD POSSIBLY BEAR THE AGONY THAT WAS AHEAD. MINUTES, HOURS, DAYS OF EXCRUCIATING PAIN, THE KIND THAT REACHES YOU EVEN WHEN YOU'RE ASLEEP.

Pain had been a part of my life for twenty years, ever since I was diagnosed with neurofibromatosis in my early teens. This baffling disorder causes tumors to grow in my head, clinging to the long nerves under my skin, tenacious as leeches. Although benign, the tumors must be removed surgically or they can damage the nerves. But every time they're operated on, they come back again, larger and more painful than before.

Now I had thirty days before my next round of surgery, thirty days of trying to cope with the pain. Normally I could take medication for relief, but not this time.

That very afternoon I had met with the surgeon who would perform the operation. "Roberta," he explained, "I know the pills you've been taking have aspirin in them. You'll have to stop using them until after the surgery. They create too much risk of hemorrhaging."

As a nurse, I understood and nodded. Inside I cringed. Even while taking this medication, the only effective one for me, I had days of agony. There were times when the short walk from the hospital parking lot to my office was like rolling a boulder up a mountain. Making my rounds, I pasted on a smile and counted the minutes until the medicine took hold, trying to concentrate on my patients' aches and pains instead. While catching up on paperwork, I shut my office door, dimmed the lights, plugged my ears with Kleenex, and wrote, holding an ice bag to my head. I kept a trash can by my desk for when I needed to vomit.

I can't possibly go that long without medication, I thought. I wouldn't be able to function. I would go mad from the pain. Now, at 2:00 AM, I was having my first glimpse of what it would be like. I staggered to the bathroom, doused a washcloth in cold water, and held it to my eye, hoping to relieve the throbbing.

My whole life had been controlled by pain. The places I went, the career I chose, the friends I made. Once, just after I was diagnosed, I fainted in class while making a speech. *I will never take another class that requires public speaking*, I told myself. Anything to avoid the embarrassment.

The pain absorbed so much of my time and energy. It was isolating. I declined invitations to parties because I was afraid I'd feel too sick to go. I rarely formed friendships with people my own age because I feared they wouldn't understand my lack of energy or my having to change plans. I turned down professional opportunities. What if I couldn't handle the workload? What if the pain got too bad?

Still, nothing could be as bad as what I faced now. Thirty days without effective medication. Thirty days of unrelieved suffering. "Dear God," I spoke to the gloom, "what am I going to do now?"

Praise Him, came the answer. Praise Him? That was so contrary to my normal impulses, so contrary to my anger for being made to suffer, that I was shocked. How could I praise Him? Most of my prayer time was spent asking for help.

I went into the kitchen and got an ice pack out of the freezer. Sinking back on my bed, I held it against my face. In the darkness of the room, with the glow of the clock turning over the minutes as they passed, one by one, I thought again of the days ahead. The urge returned: Make it thirty days of praise. I closed my eyes. How would I do that?

An image of Harriet Love, my piano teacher, came to me. I had started taking lessons because I feared the tumors would take away my eyesight. Music would be one comfort left to me. I loved sitting next to Harriet at the piano bench, admiring the roses she picked from her garden. We began our Tuesday evening sessions with a prayer, then I put aside the pressures of work and illness to concentrate on Bach, Clementi, or Chopin. For that one hour every week, my life was filled with light.

I flipped on my bedside lamp, grabbed a note card from the night-stand drawer, and scribbled a few lines to her. "Thank you, Harriet, for our wonderful lessons and the time we have together in prayer. You are a godsend." The pain didn't go away, but for a little while I was able to get away from it and outside of myself. *I'll send her the note in the morning.*

Despite the sleepless night, I went to work with a renewed sense of purpose. "Praise Him," I told myself. Now I had a way to do that—focusing on the people God had brought into my life to ease its sorrows and strains.

Logging on to my computer, I found a memo from my coworker Barbara. Another person to be thankful for. I belonged to a computer prayer group she had started. I penned her my appreciation on an-other note card, then left it under the candy dish on her desk. When I ran into her in the hall she exclaimed, "You don't know what that note meant to me!" Funny, why had I never thanked her before?

The response was so satisfying that I looked for other people to thank as the days passed, and to each I wrote a note. My hairdresser had come up with a new hairstyle for me, bringing my bangs around my glasses, which disguised the bulges from the tumors. When I looked better, I felt better. And that's what I wrote her, praising God as I penned the letter.

I recalled all the help my friend Jeanne had given me in nursing school. After classes I had gone to her house and played with her kids while she tutored me in chemistry. I hadn't seen her in years, but I wrote her a note. "Thanks for your friendship. Without you, I never would have passed chemistry, let alone gotten an A on the final."

I started writing to people who were almost strangers. The piano salesman who found me a really good buy on a Steinway grand and took my old Kawai as a trade-in. Then there was the sympathetic optician. I was having problems getting lenses and frames that fit my face. One afternoon when I went to his shop, at my wit's end, he said reassuringly, "You're not going to leave here until we get this problem fixed." And we did.

Emboldened, I even took to writing several authors whose work I admired. *Why would they want to hear from me?* I thought. And then I reminded myself that thanking them was part of praising God. Their books and articles had brought so much pleasure to my life.

But as I expanded the circle of people I was grateful for, I stopped receiving responses to my letters. For instance, I wrote to my junior-high home economics teacher, Mrs. Barrett. What a wonder she was! Instead of forcing us to sew the same boring shifts, she allowed us to choose our own designs—"as long as I can hear those scissors crunch," she said. When I came up with the idea of having a fashion show, the class sewing dresses for the teachers, she embraced it wholeheartedly. "You made me feel like I could do anything," I wrote her, thanking God for Mrs. Barrett.

I waited and waited for an answer from her. All the while, the pain continued. I sat at my desk with an ice pack, trash can nearby. At home, I lay on the family room sofa for hours, the blinds drawn, soothing music on the CD player, a sachet of fragrant herbs on my face. Of course, I knew it was unreasonable of me to expect an immediate response. Then I realized: That's not why I was writing. The prayers and praise were enough. It was the act of praying, not the outcome, that was helping.

By the time Mrs. Barrett contacted me, the praise therapy had made a permanent difference in my outlook. Instead of dwelling on my pain, letting it isolate me, the notes I wrote showed me the connections I had with so many people, from my hairdresser to the checkout man at Convenient Food Mart.

I discovered I could praise God silently through the normal routine of a day. I printed the names of people I was grateful for on yellow Post-it Notes and stuck them all over: next to the computer screen, on the dashboard, on the refrigerator. When I felt the familiar throbbing in my head, I concentrated on one of the names and said a prayer. At work, during a meeting that seemed interminable, I mentally went around the table and looked for one thing in each person I was thankful for, and prayed. Concentrated praying. Although I was battling a disease that was beyond my power to change, I felt less of a victim. My life belonged to me again.

Yes, there were moments when praise took a back burner to doubt and my pain seemed unendurable. But always I returned to thanksgiving, to prayer. In the end, the pain—the very thing that had threatened to separate me from God—brought me closer to Him.

Thirty days went quickly. My surgery was successful, and afterward I went back on my medication. By then I'd found another treatment that worked, a spiritual one. Pain will always be with me; so will God. He is more powerful than any suffering, and when I praise Him, I feel His love drawing me near, closer to Him than to anything else, even pain.

Before and After
by Dave Kostelnik

I THOUGHT THINGS COULDN'T GET ANY WORSE WHEN MY WIFE FILED FOR DIVORCE THIRTEEN YEARS AGO. MY WHOLE LIFE FELL APART. WE HAD TO SELL OUR HOUSE, AND I WOUND UP LIVING IN MY WORK TRUCK FOR A MONTH WHILE THE DIVORCE BECAME FINAL. SHE MOVED TO FLORIDA, TAKING OUR ELEVEN-YEAR-OLD DAUGHTER, CODY, WITH HER, WHILE TWELVE-YEAR-OLD JASON STAYED WITH ME. I RENTED A TEMPORARY ROOM ABOVE A SCRAP-METAL GARAGE, A TWO-FLOOR WALK-UP THAT SEEMED TO GET BLEAKER AND BLEAKER EVERY DAY.

I hit rock bottom one night in an Arby's. Jason was at a friend's for the night and I was eating alone when a young family slid into the booth across from mine. They bowed their heads to say grace, seeming to glow in the tangerine light of the big Arby's cowboy-hat sign outside the window. Then the kids tore into their meals and pulled out prizes. "Daddy," their voices rang, "can you put the pieces together?"

"Eat first," he said. "Play later."

The kids bent over their food, and the parents grinned at each other. I got up and started out the door. From my truck, I sat staring at them; they were the picture-perfect family, and I was a guy with my life in a mess. My heart sank as low and gray as a snow squall over Lake Michigan.

I didn't want to go back to my empty apartment with its chipped windowsills and uneven floor. I drove the long way through town, wishing I could hear the voice of my daughter. But instead of calling her in Florida, I dropped coins into a pay phone and dialed my pastor.

"Pastor?" I said, my voice wavering. "It's Dave Kostelnik. The carpenter. Could you pray with me, please, for a minute?"

After we finished, he reminded me, "Dave, everything looks better after a good night's sleep. Tomorrow you can start rebuilding your life."

So I went home, collapsed in bed, and slept straight through till dawn.

Pastor was right. Things did get better. The pain began to wear off. Yet some days it seemed as if I would never completely stop hurting, that my life would always be an unfixable mess. *God*, I would ask, *will I ever feel whole again?*

Spring arrived, and the days hummed with work. But my nights still stalled out. One day, a little before Easter, I noticed a House for Sale sign in the front window of Mr. Mehlhose's ice-cream parlor. An arrow pointed at a decrepit green giant of a Victorian squatting next door. I didn't think much of it until I got to my first job that day.

We were roofing, and I could see the budding trees and the houses and sunny yards of the neighborhood. I could hear hammering and the whine of power saws. Our town was going through major renovations. If old houses weren't up to code, they would be torn down. On the good side, that meant employment for me; on the bad side, it meant the house I'd seen for sale would be red-tagged before long and lost for good.

After work, I went back to the old doomed house and sat on the front steps, trying to imagine what it would be like for Jason and me to live there, what it might have been like to grow up in the house when it was in its prime. I watched families down the street coming home for dinner. I put my hands to a window and looked in at the sad, empty rooms and blank walls. I walked around the yard and fence, circling the house and inspecting everything up close. Then I crossed the street for the long view. To my relief, the foundation lay squarely, and the roof sat upright in the half-light. "You remind me of me, house," I said out loud. "We'll have to see about this."

The next day I went to Mr. Mehlhose's ice-cream parlor and asked him if he would show me around the house next door, the one for sale.

"Sure thing, Dave." He closed up his shop and unlocked the back door of the house. "She was built in 1903 and has been in the family for years," he told me as he switched on the lights. "You can see I updated the kitchen and the dining room some, probably for the worse, but still—" We moved on. "Got the sitting room here," he said, "and the library's through there."

"Nice woodwork," I told him. "Lots of memories, I bet."

"That'd be a safe bet," he said and smiled.

"What's under the linoleum?" I asked.

"Pine, I think. But the rest of the floors are oak." Mr. Mehlhose waved his hand toward the living room and walked me through the cellar and the upstairs: the bedrooms, the closets, the attic. I kept a running count of all the problems with this old house—from the roof and windows to the plumbing and furnace. I added up all the fixes, all the hours, all the pieces that would have to be repaired or replaced. On the staircase, I ran my hands along the curved oak railing and admired the ornate spindles, calculating how long it would take to strip, sand, and refinish each one.

When Mr. Mehlhose clicked off the light and pulled the door closed behind us, I again felt a strange kinship with the house. "I'd like to buy it," I said, "to fix it up and live here."

After the legal work was done, Jason and I got the keys and moved into our new home with Snoopy, our basset hound. We spent the summer cleaning the yard and putting a new roof on the house, scraping and sanding off the old green paint, priming and then giving her a fresh coat of gray with cranberry accents. Cody came to visit and helped too. Inside me, little by little, those deep shadows of despair were fading.

Fall carried the process indoors, and I started the slow and tedious work of going room by room. *Give me patience, Lord*, I kept praying. It took me all winter to renovate just one bedroom. Yet I felt myself recuperating as I restored the old place. Maybe both of us could be made whole and new again.

From time to time, Mr. Mehlhose stopped by to cheer along our progress or relay a compliment about the improvements on the house. He brought snapshots one evening, a whole scrapbook of the house over the years. "It used to be beautiful, Dave, didn't it?"

"And look at what used to be there," I said. "A front porch." I traced my finger over a photo labeled 1907, following the long porch that ran the width of the house. That night I wandered outside and felt the old clapboards for the notches that had joined the porch to the house. And they were there, like scars.

Easter marked a year in our new home, and that spring I tore out the drop ceiling in the kitchen, brought in period cabinets and a stove and kept tearing, patching, mending, and rebuilding. With work and God's grace, as well as a little luck, things seemed to be falling into place both for the house and for me. I was able to spend lots of good times with my kids and still have the time and energy to work at tasks that made me proud. I found French doors at an auction, and the flooring under the linoleum was magnificent—wide tongue-and-groove pinewood.

Then someone set me up on a blind date with a woman named Mary. Her husband had died two years earlier, and she was raising a young son. On our first date, Mary told me that she was rebuilding her life from the inside out.

"Boy," I said, smiling, "do I have something to show you!"

A year later, we were married. Together we bent side by side with our kids at the oak banister, sanding dirt and grime from each spindle. Top to bottom, it took eleven years to renovate the house, right down to the new porch that now runs the width of the front. We know every last inch of the place, every last pipe and brick, every mood and season, every before and after. And for me personally, as that house was restored, so was I.

When we learned our house was registered as a historic site in Wyandotte, Michigan, we threw a great party, a celebration as much for ourselves as for our home. After all, we'd put our lives back together with the same tools as we'd used on the house—love and faith, unstinting work and care—and, if I do say so myself, both our house and our hearts have traveled quite a ways from rock bottom thanks to God's grace.

22.

Transformed
by Rebecca Ashburn

EASTER MORNING I WOKE TO THE SHRILL OF MY ALARM CLOCK. I HIT THE OFF SWITCH AND SANK BACK ON MY PILLOW. OUTSIDE MY WINDOW, THE WHOLE WORLD SEEMED TO SING OF SPRING. *EXCEPT ME*, I THOUGHT. EVEN THOUGH IT HAD BEEN A WHILE SINCE MY DIVORCE, I COULDN'T SEEM TO GET PAST IT. WOULD I EVER FEEL JOYOUS AGAIN?

"Mama, get up!" my seven-year-old daughter, Elise, cried, jumping on my bed. "We have to get to church!"

That was exactly what I was dreading. There had been too many reminders of my marriage at our old church, so Elise and I joined a new one. She'd adjusted fine but I felt out of place there, as I did pretty much everywhere since the divorce. I knew seeing the rest of the congregation at Easter service with their families would only remind me how I'd failed with my own.

At least put on a happy face for Elise, I told myself as I climbed out of bed. "All right, sweetie, let's get dressed."

Twenty minutes later, Elise was standing by the door, holding three drooping daffodils, the stems carefully wrapped in a damp paper towel. Her Sunday school teacher had asked the class to bring flowers to church for the Easter cross, and yesterday Elise had found three lonely daffodils poking out of the soil in our yard. She'd picked them right then and there. "I was afraid we'd forget later," she'd said.

Now Elise smiled at me from the doorway. "Don't my flowers look great, Mama?" she asked.

At church, she proudly presented her three bedraggled blooms to the women in charge of decorating the Easter cross. They were busy arranging the children's flowers, most as sorry-looking as Elise's, in the holes of the chicken wire covering the rough wooden cross. To me, the whole thing looked as if it didn't belong in church any more than I did.

I took my seat just as organ music signaled the beginning of the procession. I turned to watch Elise walk down the aisle with the other kids when I caught sight of the cross. One large, red poppy rested at the center and daffodils and narcissus radiated out in gorgeous waves of gold and white, sprinkled with lilac, japonica, and forsythia. The effect was stunning. All those wilted flowers together created a transformation. Each had its place in the cross. I looked at Elise. She was beaming. And for the first time in many months, I felt a joyous smile blossoming on my own face too.

23.

The Illness I Couldn't Allow

by Pam Rosewell Moore

EACH TIME I SPEAK TO A CHURCH GROUP ABOUT MY STRUGGLE WITH CLINICAL DEPRESSION, I'LL INVARIABLY SEE A LOOK OF DOUBT CROSS SOMEONE'S FACE. I KNOW WHAT SHE'S THINKING: DEPRESSION ONLY PLAGUES THOSE WHO HAVE NOT SURRENDERED THEMSELVES COMPLETELY TO GOD. I USED TO THINK THE SAME THING. I DIDN'T UNDERSTAND HOW A COMMITTED CHRISTIAN COULD EVER BECOME DEPRESSED.

When I was growing up in England, I'd often stand by the window on winter evenings, watching the snow fall. Quiet, enveloping—it reminded me of the gloom I couldn't seem to shake. My brother and sister had an optimism and enthusiasm I didn't share. Yet I tried my best to cover up the dark feelings and put on a cheerful face.

From the age of five I had believed in the sacrifice Jesus had made for me, but it wasn't until I was twenty-one that I wholly put my trust in Him. That moment would define the rest of my life. I'd always been terrified to leave my home and family, yet I was led to Africa to do mission work. I was afraid of speaking in public, yet I was guided to help advocate the cause of the church in communist countries. I very much wanted to be married, yet I came to be a caregiver and companion to Dutch missionary Corrie ten Boom, who had shared with millions how God sustained her through the horrors of a Nazi concentration camp. I stayed with her for the last seven years of her life, while she was ill.

Shortly after Corrie's death, my mother died. These two losses, so close together, left me emotionally and physically drained. But two years later I found new joy and strength when I met Carey after a talk I gave in Waco, Texas, about my past work. Eight months later, I married him. I was forty-two. Soon after, I became the director of the intercessory prayer ministry at Dallas Baptist University.

I immersed myself in my new life, yet tiredness nagged at me. It was a common complaint in my journal. But I pressed on with a packed schedule of work and speaking engagements. At one talk, I met Deana, a counselor. We became close, and she worried about all the pressure I put on myself. She even suggested I talk to her or another counselor about it.

"Talking to you would make anyone feel better, I'm sure," I said to Deana, "but isn't God the only counselor we need?"

"Emotions can sometimes overwhelm us, even with God in our lives," she replied.

I couldn't see how that was possible. There was one student, in her late twenties, whom I had prayed with numerous times about her search for a husband. She insisted she had put the matter in God's hands but was still filled with desperation. One day after praying, she looked up at me and said, "I have never felt so depressed."

"You have to surrender yourself completely to God," I insisted. "Only then will you break free of this sadness." A veil dropped over her eyes. "I'm trying but—" I told her again how confident I was that the Lord would work wonders in her life, if she let Him.

After all, I reminded myself, I had seen Him do so with many of the young people I'd prayed with. It was fulfilling to see that happen. I loved my work. And I loved my husband. But my tiredness persisted and sometimes in the evenings, sitting side by side with Carey in our blue easy chairs, reading the paper, I'd feel a whisper of that melancholy I remembered from my childhood.

Then Carey was diagnosed with cancer. He started chemotherapy but the doctors couldn't make any guarantees. The thought of losing the man I had waited so long to find was almost unbearable, but as far as I knew how, I surrendered him to God. I wanted to take care of him, as I had Corrie. I needed to. But looking at his face threw me into a tailspin. *Will he suffer terribly? Will I be able to help him? What if he dies?*

Carey remained upbeat. The strain of trying to match his mood drained me. At work, I frequently closed my office door and cried. Once, a school trustee started talking to me about his mother's illness and I broke down right in front of him.

"I don't do things like that," I wrote in my journal that night before bed. "What's wrong with me?"

Maybe I just need rest, I thought. But I kept waking up in the wee hours of the morning and getting caught in a tangle of fearful thoughts. I'd lie awake listening to the slow rhythm of Carey's breathing until dawn.

One day we were preparing to go to a church picnic. I was in the kitchen wrapping sandwiches when Carey walked in. "Are those sandwiches ready to take to the car yet?"

"No, I'm still working on them," I snapped. Carey stared at me, surprised.

"I barely got any sleep last night," I railed. I went on and on.

"I'm sorry," he said. "Take your time. There's no need to hurry." I was horrified at my outburst. *What am I doing?* I thought. *Carey needs my love more than ever and I'm being cross with him about stupid, silly things.*

Carey was patient, forgiving, but I knew he too wondered at my behavior. As always, I turned to my Bible for help, but I could barely get through a verse without anxious thoughts taking over.

One afternoon during lunchtime at work, I flipped through a magazine. I saw an article about depression that included a checklist of symptoms. I checked off the boxes in my head. Fatigue. Sleeplessness. Irritability. Inability to concentrate. I closed the magazine and resolved that I would not be so weak. But more and more I felt overwhelmed by an inability to cope with life.

Then came New Year's. "Let's each go over our journals and review the past year," Carey said, "then pray about this new one."

I watched him walk down the hall to the study, his hair almost gone from the chemo.

I pulled my journal out of my dresser drawer and ruffled the pages. I didn't want to relive the past year. I wanted to think of the future even less. *Maybe this will be the last new year Carey and I celebrate together.*

Again came those negative thoughts I couldn't escape. Why wasn't I able to turn the future over to the Lord? How had this pervasive pessimism taken over my life? Suddenly I thought of the lonely young woman I'd counseled years before. Is this what she'd felt like? As though she had done everything she knew how and it still wasn't good enough?

I felt the familiar tears and went to wash my face. Looking at myself in the mirror, I seemed to see the years stretching out before me, long and empty and hopeless. *I must be depressed.* I had always believed I could do all things through Christ who strengthens me, but then why, when I needed that strength more than ever, could I not receive it? Why did I feel so weak?

I joined Carey in the living room. I wanted him to hold me but the fear and sadness had me too tightly in their grip. What would he think of me if I told him I was depressed? What would everyone think? That my faith was lacking?

I would have to see my doctor. Carey and I held hands to pray and I closed my eyes. How many prayers I had said for others, yet all I could manage now was, *Lord, please help me.*

Two weeks later, I sat very still in the examining room as my doctor explained what was making me feel the way I did. "You have a chemical imbalance in your brain, Pam. I'm going to prescribe a medication. It's a hormone that regulates mood. It'll help, but you have to get plenty of rest too."

Could the answer be in a pill? Would I be letting God down by taking it, instead of relying on my faith?

When I got home, I told Carey everything.

"Pam, I had no idea you were feeling terrible. If this medicine will help, then yes, of course I think you should take it." He reached for my hand. "Why didn't you tell me?"

"I didn't want it to come between us."

"How could it? I love you."

I knew that. And I knew God loved me too. I wanted so much to be well again.

I started taking the medicine my doctor had prescribed. Within days, I felt some of the terrible ache that had haunted me ease. *How could this be?* I wondered.

Carey helped me find articles and books about depression and they described the way I felt to a T. They stressed the biological roots of the illness: just as a broken leg causes physical pain, a chemical imbalance in the brain causes the emotional pain of depression.

As I continued to get better, I worked harder to make up for the times I'd felt too low to concentrate. Soon I was more overwhelmed than ever. After one hard day at the office, I felt totally spent. As soon as I got home, I slumped into my blue chair and called my friend Deana. She came over and made me some hot tea. "You have to slow down, Pam," she said. "Have some quiet time."

I sighed. "I'm afraid to. If I don't keep busy, maybe the sadness will come back."

"It's part of you. You have to deal with it."

She was right. I'd spent my whole life denying it. I'd always worked in God's service. Now I had to stop and heal with God's help.

I took a leave of absence from work and began counseling sessions with Deana.

I decided I had to simplify things. Carey and I moved to a rural community outside Dallas. When I returned to work, it was on a part-time basis, as the university's Director of Spiritual Life. Fears about Carey's health no longer had the same power over me. I learned to stroll, to rest, to begin to focus on prayer again. The sadness that had clouded my life gradually faded. Then one day Carey's doctor announced his cancer was in remission. I joined my husband on our back porch that evening and we held each other close.

Every sufferer experiences the pain of depression in a different way. What leads me to share my experience again and again is the young student whose pain I didn't understand and the millions of others out there who are still suffering in silent shame. Depressive illness can happen to anybody. It happened to me. But through it, I came to know and love God in a way I'd never imagined.

24.

Messengers in the Night
by Betsi Fox

I THREW MY DUFFEL BAG OF CLOTHES, A COUPLE OF CANS OF SODA, AND MY RIFLE ONTO THE BOTTOM OF THE SKIFF AND DRAGGED IT INTO THE WATER. BRUISER, OUR NINETY-POUND GERMAN SHEPHERD, SCRAMBLED INTO THE BOW AS I CHECKED THE GAS AND MADE SURE THE EXTRA TANK WAS FULL.

For just a moment I hesitated. I'd never taken a boat this small into the choppy open water off the Alaska coast. The skiff was a twelve-foot fiberglass affair with an outboard motor that buzzed like a sick bee. The boat didn't even have oars, just an old snow shovel to paddle with in a pinch. But shucks, I'd lived alone in the bush, caught my own food, faced down grizzly bears—how hard could a little boat trip be?

I did a balancing act as I tugged at the starter cord. The engine was old and temperamental, but it finally caught and off we puttered. My four-year-old daughter, Becca, and the other kids at our makeshift school waved good-bye from the shore as I rounded the point. Off by myself at last! It was a sunny July day, the sea calm after three weeks of nonstop wind and rain. I leaned back against my duffel, drinking in the solitude and the sunlight as we crept past a chain of uninhabited spruce-clad islands, Bruiser barking at every drifting log and floating otter.

I didn't know how long going back to our home island would take. Becca and I had always come here in my husband's big fishing trawler—just over a two-hour trip with the powerful diesel engine. He'd brought the skiff along so I could poke around in the sheltered cove of the island where the school was located. Many fishermen's families lived, as we did, on isolated islands and we solved the problem of school by bringing our children together on the island with the largest cabin. Mothers took turns teaching, three or four days at a stretch. But no sooner had my latest stint begun than stormy weather set in, marooning me for three weeks, the only adult with fifteen cooped-up kids. When the weather finally broke and my replacement arrived, I was ready to take off for home on anything that floated.

Now we were making slower progress than I'd reckoned on. We'd gone barely a third of the way when the motor gave an ominous sputter and died.

Out of gas already! I'd have to stop at the small town of Sitka, our local "metropolis," to refuel. I hooked up the spare tank, then pulled the starter cord. Nothing. I tried again. A cough, then silence. I took a break, cracked the top of a soda, shared some with Bruiser, then tackled the outboard again. Rocking the boat in my exertions, I spilled the rest of the can. When at last the engine turned over, I celebrated with my second and last pop, again sharing it with Bruiser.

Four hours later it was getting dark and I was starting to worry. I should have sighted Sitka by now! Had I taken a wrong turn among the maze of islands? The temperature was dropping fast, the frigid Alaska night coming on. I pulled a jacket from my duffel bag and wondered how much gas was left.

So typical of me—in a rush to go off by myself, all my life preferring unknown dangers ahead to what lay behind.

It had started in my childhood in Ohio with my stepmother and the harsh, judgmental God she'd held over me. A rigid, sanctimonious woman, she showed a pious face to the world and saved her violent rages for me. On my nineteenth birthday, ten years ago, I had put a knapsack and a sleeping bag on my back and hitchhiked as far as I could go, fearing every mile that the angry policeman of a God she'd preached at me was hot on my heels.

It took me thirteen days to thumb five thousand miles. I ended up in Alaska and have made it my home ever since, marrying and raising a family on a remote island twelve miles from the nearest neighbor.

I was accustomed to roughing it, but this boat trip had become more than I bargained for. I was cold, thirsty, and ravenously hungry by the time I saw the lights of Sitka in the distance. I groaned with relief. Moments later I heard an all-too-familiar sputter. The engine coughed twice and went dead. The last gas was gone—and I was still miles from town.

Keep calm, I told myself. *You've managed alone before.*

If I could make it to land, any land, I'd simply build a fire and wait for morning when I could signal a passing fishing boat. I grabbed the shovel and stroked as hard as I could in the direction of the nearest island. Its shadowy outline only got farther away. The tide was going out! The current was too strong to row against, even if I'd had oars.

Bruiser! My big dog was a powerful swimmer. If I tied the bow-rope around his neck, would he be able to tow the boat to shore? I secured the rope around him all right, but when I tried to push him from the boat he gave a low whine that said all too clearly, "No way am I going in that freezing water."

There was nothing to do but watch the lights of Sitka grow dimmer as the slap of the waves carried us into the open sea. I dug out every warm thing I had in the duffel and hunkered down. Surely in the morning a fishing boat would see us!

I did see boats the next day, but they were far in the distance—wooden specks on the vast blue ocean. I tied my red bathrobe to the end of the shovel and waved it and shouted till I had no voice left.

There were two bullets in my rifle. Desperate, I fired them both, knowing even as I did that the noise of the boats' engines would most likely drown out the sound.

Farther and farther from land we drifted. The sun beat down on the open skiff, cracking my lips, cheeks, forehead. I knew better than to drink seawater, but that afternoon I got so hot that I splashed some on my face. It only blistered the cracked skin.

Night came again, then dawn. That third day I saw boats on the horizon, but I had no strength to wave my shovel and no voice to call with. As the third night at sea came on, I thought, *I'm going to die.* "If I should die before I wake—" The words of the prayer my stepmother made me say on my knees each night, standing over me with a switch in case I left any out, came back to me. "—I pray the Lord my soul to take."

No! Anything but that! I hadn't prayed at all in ten years, least of all for my soul to go to my stepmother's vindictive God—a God as angry as she was. I'd come to Alaska to escape—gone where neither she nor He could find me. Bruiser and I would die out here by ourselves and that was that.

I must have fallen asleep on the cramped floor of the skiff because I was awakened by icy water splashing on my face. There was an explosive exhalation, followed by something scraping softly against the side of the boat.

Struggling to sit up straight, I stared out over the moonlit sea.

And then I saw them. Great black-and-white shapes gliding past. Now on the other side, circling round. A pod of orca whales, surrounding and dwarfing my tiny craft. One, two, four, seven—nine of the colossal creatures!

Bruiser, who would ordinarily bark at anything that moved, sat quietly beside me, his head in my lap.

A few yards away, one of the giants breached, then dove. The whale's flukes were bigger than the boat, yet they left barely a ripple on the sea's placid surface. The merest flick of that tail would certainly have capsized us.

The whale breached again, spouting water through its blowhole with a great whoosh but again barely rocking the skiff. The next time one of the orcas brushed up against the boat, I reached out to touch its smooth skin. It stayed close, as though it liked to be petted.

All through the night, the pod circled the boat, calling out to each other—and to me too, I imagined—with squeaks and whistles. *What are they saying?* I wondered. *Are they concerned at finding a fellow creature alone? Staying near to keep me company?* Adrift at sea, distant as I'd ever managed to be, I was confronted with a nearness I trembled to name.

Who had sent me these giant creatures to give the lie to the word alone? I wondered. The answer was too large, too obvious to miss. How could I have let my stepmother's anger blind me to the truth that breathed in the water all around? God had pursued me—I'd been absolutely right about that. But not to punish me. Sometimes, I thought, when the distance gets too great, God has to send really big ambassadors to bring us back to Him.

Gently rocked by the circling whales, I, at last, fell asleep. I woke the next morning to Bruiser's barking and the *chug-chug-chug* of an engine.

A fishing boat was coming toward me. I looked around for the pod of whales. They were gone, but in their place was the assurance that God will pursue us to the ends of the earth and beyond, not to condemn but to surround us with love.

25.

The Lost Shoes

by Evelyn Gaines

IT SEEMS ABSURD AND ALMOST SACRILEGIOUS TO SAY IT, BUT WHENEVER I GO BACK OVER MY STRUGGLE TO RETAIN MY FAITH IN GOD, I SEE IN MY MIND'S EYE A PAIR OF SHOES—OLD SHOES, SCUFFED AT THE TOES AND WORN DOWN AT THE HEELS. I THINK OF THEM OFTEN, WONDERING WHAT BECAME OF THEM AFTER THEY WERE DISCARDED IN THAT DARK ALLEYWAY IN PITTSBURGH THREE YEARS AGO.

Those shoes led a man and a woman back to God.

When I married Jack [name has been changed to protect identity], he was a rising young executive with a fuel firm whose work entailed social contacts with prospective customers.

I must have seemed very young, very naive to a man like Jack. I was a schoolteacher, whereas he had traveled extensively and mingled with all kinds of people. He wanted to get along, and at thirty-two he thought he knew the answer: "You have to get to know the right people," he'd say.

Jack always attended church with me, but it was only a courtesy; religion had no real meaning for him.

In my parents' home, on the living room mantel, the Bible had been almost like a family reference book; one that our father had taught us, held the answer to successful, everyday living. But, with Jack, my new home now lacked this comforting reassurance, and I worried about the years ahead.

Shortly after our marriage, Jack's firm transferred him to another city. To make business contacts, they paid his dues to various social clubs in that city. Our life began to revolve about a crowd that seemed bent upon amusement only, and that looked upon liquor as a necessary stimulant to set the party spinning. I couldn't drink, never had. It wasn't long before Jack went out alone to these parties and I knew we were growing apart. He stayed at the office as late as possible, and I never knew when he would be home—seven, eight, ten o'clock—always well fortified with cocktails.

Then, one night, the inevitable happened. He didn't return, or even go through the pretense of phoning some excuse. By now, I think I'd lost even my belief in the power of prayer. I prayed purely out of habit. I had been on my knees for some time when the phone rang. A woman's voice came over the wire. "Are you Mrs. Gaines?"

"Yes," I replied.

There was a pause and then the gentle voice continued hesitantly, "Has your husband been ill lately?"

"Why, no-o. What's happened?"

"Well—he was picked up unconscious a little while ago in front of my house. I think the police have taken him to a hospital—"

He wasn't ill; he was drunk. I bailed him out of jail and he was ashamed and conscience-stricken. All his assurance, his self-confidence, seemed to have forsaken him, and when that happens to a man like Jack, to whom else can he turn but God? But Jack didn't believe in God.

It is painful to write down what I now must, even after eight years have passed. I hadn't the faintest clue that anything was wrong when he came home one summer evening and told me the company had pushed his vacation two weeks ahead, although when he said we hadn't enough funds to make our customary motor trip, I was a little surprised. Then one evening toward the end of those two weeks, Jack paused in his pacing of the floor.

"Evie," he said, "I must tell you something and, God help me, I don't know how to do it. The company—has let me go."

"Jack, why—?"

I thought I already knew the answer—his drinking—and I wasn't prepared for the words that seemed forced from him.

"They've let me go…for embezzlement."

Embezzlement! My mind didn't grasp it for a moment, but when the full realization came, my heart refused to accept it. Jack, a thief!

That was the closest I ever came to losing my last vestige of faith in God. Yet, so deeply ingrained had been the teaching of prayer that, as I went about the household tasks, I still found my lips moving, pleading with God for an answer to the muddle of our lives.

Because Jack had been with the firm so long, he was given the opportunity to make restitution. Even though it meant years of debt I was thankful. It was as though God had given him another chance. Besides, I knew now Jack was finally aware of the desperate need to rid himself of the alcohol habit.

My proud young husband was gone from me now. In his place stood a man, prematurely gray, with disillusioned eyes and hands that shook. Eventually, he obtained another position and I went back to teaching and some freelance writing. There was no other way for us to pay back our debt.

There were times, as is the way with alcoholics, when Jack would sink into fits of depression that would last a week or longer.

Holidays seemed to be his worst nemesis: time on his hands.

One Easter, thinking to make it easier for him, I suggested a trip to Pittsburgh. We took my young niece who had come to us for her vacation. There was an Easter play for children that I was anxious for Jeanie to see, and at the hotel Jack secured the last two available tickets. He insisted Jeanie and I use them. He would, he said, pick up a magazine, go back to the hotel, and read.

"Besides," he added, looking at me with a smile, "you don't approve of my old shoes."

He had forgotten to change before leaving home and I had chided him. Jack had always been an immaculate dresser, but with the loss of his own self-respect, he seemed at times to be losing interest in his outward appearance as well.

After the theater, Jeanie and I went directly to our room. Jack had a single room across the corridor and I paused outside it and called his name softly. But there was no answer, so we decided he was asleep.

Around nine-thirty the next morning I arose, dressed quietly, and tiptoed across the hall. Jack opened the door and I noticed the air smelled heavy of stale liquor.

Jack was still in his pajamas and he looked sick. As he turned to move back toward the bed, I noticed he was limping.

"Jack, are you all right?"

I took his arm, steadying him as he sank down on the side of the bed and put his head in his hands. "Oh, Evie, I've been such a fool."

I bent down to draw his hands away from his face and that's when I noticed his feet—they were grimy and caked with dried blood.

"Oh, God," I prayed, "give me strength to face whatever I must."

Jack reached out a hand and pulled me down beside him.

"The old story, Evie," he said heavily. "I began to make the rounds of the bars right after you and Jeanie left me. Between drinks, I recall standing in front of a store window full of shoes. They were clean and shiny and I told myself it would please you if I bought new ones. But first I must get rid of my old ones. In my befuddled state I walked down a nearby alley and, behind a building, discarded my old shoes. Only when I got back to the shop did I realize that it was closed."

He paused and looked at me out of bloodshot eyes, trying so valiantly to smile.

"It was then," he said, "that I realized I was shoeless. I turned and made my way back down the alley—but the shoes were gone.... Perhaps it was the wrong alley. I kept on searching; up one dark, cluttered lane after another; miles and miles of gloomy, squalid alleys filled with trash and garbage. I knew now I was lost—hopelessly lost, and fear began to claw at me. *If only*, I thought, *I can find my way back to Evie*, and so I kept on searching all through that lone, dark night. The shoes were forgotten now. It was you I must find; my way back to you. But that seemed impossible and then it came to me. *Perhaps, if I prayed to Evie's God—*"

He studied his hands that twisted so restlessly upon his knees. "That must seem really funny to you, Evie—me, appealing to God. But it wasn't funny for, as I was stumbling along one of those dim, shabby streets into which I had groped my way, I saw a light approaching. It was a cruising cabby but to me it was God, answering my prayer. Suddenly I was rational enough to see it was a way of getting back to you."

Jack turned and looked toward the window. "It was dawn when I reached this room. The light was just breaking over those dark rooftops. Do you know what I've been doing, Evie?"

I shook my head.

"Just kneeling there watching it; watching God sending the glory of His light down upon all of us, the just, like you, Evie—and the unjust, like me. I guess my first prayer must have sounded pretty gauche to Him, but I just thanked Him for the light. And, Evie"—there was awe in his voice—"I have a feeling. Not one I can explain but just a feeling— that He understood."

"Jack," I said wonderingly, "that's faith! That's what He meant when He said, If ye have faith . . ."

And Jack has. It has been a lamp unto his feet, his feet which, since that night, in his search for God, have never stumbled.

The Kindness Factor
by Roberta L. Messner

A VA HOSPITAL IS A BIG PLACE. I SHOULD KNOW, I WORK IN ONE. BUT THAT MORNING IT WASN'T BIG ENOUGH. NOT WITH MY NEWLY EX-HUSBAND AND FELLOW NURSE, MARK, ROAMING THE HALLS. I'D MANAGED TO AVOID HIM FOR A FEW WEEKS SINCE OUR DIVORCE HAD BECOME FINAL, BUT NOW, THERE HE WAS, DRESSED IN HIS SCRUBS, ESCORTING A PATIENT TO THE RADIOLOGY ROOM. HE SAW ME AND SMILED. AT LEAST I THOUGHT IT WAS A SMILE. "JUST THIRTY-SIX MORE DAYS UNTIL RETIREMENT!" HE ANNOUNCED BLITHELY. MY BLOOD RAN COLD. I'D ALMOST FORGOTTEN. WHEN WE'D MARRIED TWENTY-FIVE YEARS AGO, WE'D PLANNED TO RETIRE AND TRAVEL AROUND THE WORLD RIGHT ABOUT NOW. I GUESSED THAT WAS STILL MARK'S PLAN, BUT THANKS TO HIM, IT COULDN'T BE MINE ANYMORE. NO WAY COULD I AFFORD RETIREMENT.

I tried to be civil. "So, still planning to do some traveling?" I asked.

"Moving to Alaska," he said. "Maybe do a little consulting, but for the most part, I'll just fly and live the good life."

"Fly?"

"Didn't I tell you? I bought that vintage airplane I always wanted."

No. He didn't tell me. Now my blood was boiling. Even the knowledge he'd be thousands of miles away didn't soothe me. He was going to live it up while I spent the next five years or more digging out from the financial mess he'd left me in. I stormed off before I made a scene.

The words from the Bible that Mark and I had pledged to each other on our wedding day came to mind: "Whither thou goest I will go; where thou lodgest, I will lodge." How meaningless those words had been to Mark! Maybe he could go on like nothing happened, but I couldn't!

Since I was a teenager, I'd suffered health problems that could cause debilitating pain and other complications. Stress made it worse, and living with Mark didn't help. At first, he'd made me laugh with his crazy brand of humor. He'd stood by me through all the doctor appointments and treatments. I put almost every cent I earned into paying off our house and making it beautiful. It was even featured in a few home magazines. I pictured us growing old there, together. But instead, we grew apart. Things changed.

Mark's good qualities gave way to the bad ones. He had a miserable temper, and could fly into rages over the littlest things. Bad feelings built up between us. For eight years I'd worked an extra job to get us by while he'd gone back to school for an advanced degree. Then when I mentioned that my boss urged me to consider going on disability during one of my more severe health flare-ups, Mark flew off the handle. "Wait one minute!" he yelled. "I didn't sign up for this. You're not going to up and quit your job and expect me to pick up the slack." That was the last straw. After all I'd put up with, when I needed him the most, he turned his back. I'd never forgive him for that.

Mark stayed in our house while we worked out the details of the divorce. I moved to a ramshackle log cabin. I thought I could fix it up to start anew. I tried to put a good spin on things to my friends, laughing about how I called my new home the Leaning Log because everywhere I stood in it, the uneven floor made me lean. "I'm so sorry, Roberta," they'd say. "He just treated you awful."

"No," I'd say, "we just needed to go our separate ways."

What I couldn't bear to bring up was how little I got in the divorce settlement, how the lawyers' fees and the low sale price we'd taken on our house didn't leave nearly enough to fix up the cabin. I didn't know how I'd manage. I wondered how Mark could afford his retirement. It wasn't fair!

At a checkup, my doctor said, "Your blood pressure's up, Roberta. Anything bothering you?" I started to say I was fine when all at once it came out, all the anger I'd been storing up. I told him how Mark had left me with almost nothing in the divorce, how I still had to see him at work, how it seemed he was rubbing it in my face with his quips about retirement, doing all the stuff we'd dreamed about.

Dr. Brownfield shook his head. "Stress can aggravate your condition. You know that. Take care of yourself. Eat right. Get rest. You've got to find a way to let this go."

Let it go? How? I knew the doctor was right. But I wasn't done being angry.

For a solid week afterward, I couldn't sleep. I felt myself getting more and more sick. By the weekend, I didn't know if I'd have the energy to go in to work the following Monday. I collapsed on my bed. I did the only thing I knew to do. I prayed. Not for the first time, of course, not by a long shot. But with a desperation I'd never experienced. "Lord, I know I need to let go of this," I cried out. "But how? Even when he's gone, every day at work will just remind me I have no one and he's out having the time of his life." I knew what God's answer was. *Forgive Mark. Focus on the future, not the past.* But I simply didn't know how to forgive Mark. I tried. I couldn't.

The next day at work, I could barely function. "You okay?" asked Sandy, one of the other nurses. She'd recently lost her husband. If she was asking me if I was okay, I must have looked in really bad shape.

"I'm fine," I insisted.

Sandy sat down with one of our long-term patients, Mr. Lansing. He'd once told me how seeing her was the best part of his day. I'd meant to tell Sandy that but had let it slip my mind.

At my desk I spied a box of pansy-patterned cards a student I'd once mentored had given me. An inspiration struck. I pulled one out and wrote, "Dear Sandy, you make the biggest difference in your patients' lives. I see it every day. Especially this afternoon with Mr. Lansing. He told me that he watches the clock for 8:00 AM when your shift begins. Thank you for caring so much about our veteran patients."

I gave Sandy the card. "You don't know how much this means," she said, grasping my hands tight. Seeing her smile meant a lot to me. Being thankful for a person and letting her know felt so much better than being resentful.

I decided to write "Caught in the Act of Caring" notes whenever I saw someone doing a good job or when someone brightened my day. Every time I wrote a note, it seemed my eyes were opened to new people I could give a kind word to. People I'd overlooked because I was so focused on my misery. Giving kindness was like the antidote to the poison of my resentment toward Mark. I felt energized when I came home. Enough to work on my garden at the Leaning Log, which was looking nicer every day. I potted some red geraniums and gave them out to coworkers. The day Mark left the hospital for good, I barely took note. *He's moving on with his life. I'm moving on with mine.*

"Has your diet changed?" Dr. Brownfield asked at my next appointment. My blood pressure had dropped twenty points.

"No, just my attitude," I said.

One night, home at the Leaning Log, sorting through some boxes, I came across an old anniversary card from Mark. Slowly, I opened it up. It was sweet, funny—the Mark I'd fallen in love with. At least those moments I'd always be thankful for.

Thankful for Mark? A few weeks ago, I probably would have ripped up the card. But I wasn't in the same place anymore. All my caring notes had moved me to a different place, a place of forgiveness and letting go. I didn't want resentment to rule my life anymore. "Lord," I said, "wherever Mark is right now, I forgive him. Forgiveness is how I show my love for You in return for the unending love You give me." It was strange, but the last bit of weight that seemed to sit on my shoulders lifted away.

I've heard from friends that Mark's doing well in Alaska. He's enjoying life. And it doesn't make me unhappy. Anger and resentment did. Mark can't hurt me anymore. As soon as I stopped counting my grievances, I could see my blessings. I could let go of the pain and embrace the future. My log cabin is paid in full and renovations are progressing well. My health is stable. I love my job more than ever, and my life too, free of the past.

27.

"Peace, Be Still"

by Mary Ann O'Roark

I MUST HAVE BEEN ABOUT ELEVEN YEARS OLD, BANGING OUT STORIES ON MY PORTABLE TYPEWRITER IN OUR WEST VIRGINIA BACKYARD, WHEN A SPARKLING PATCH OF LIGHT APPEARED IN THE MIDDLE OF A SENTENCE. I BLINKED, BUT INSTEAD OF GOING AWAY, THE LIGHT CHURNED INTO A DIZZYING CASCADE. THERE WAS A BUZZING IN MY TEMPLES, MY LIPS AND FINGERS TINGLED, AND I SEEMED TO BE LOOKING AT THE PAGE THROUGH A RAPIDLY TURNING KALEIDOSCOPE.

I sat paralyzed, unable to call or run for help. After about twenty minutes, the pulsing lights vanished. But I felt nauseous and disoriented. And on the right side of my head there was a sickening throb. I ran to my room and huddled in bed with a pillow over my head to block out the world spinning around me, then fell asleep. When I awoke later that afternoon, the worst of the pain was gone, and what had happened seemed like a bad dream.

But it was just the beginning. Every few months, the flashing patterns of light reappeared, followed by excruciating pain in the right side of my head and the back of my neck. If I tried to speak, my words didn't match my thoughts. The faintest light or sound made me cringe.

Why did I slip away to my room and not tell anyone? Because I was afraid—afraid of going to the doctor, afraid of seeming weird. Year after year I suffered in secret. Then, at sixteen, I was waiting at church one night for my mother to finish choir practice when the pain struck. I lay down in the pew and rested my throbbing head against the polished wood.

Often when I was in the sanctuary, I thought of the Bible stories that had always comforted me: an ailing woman reaching out to touch Christ's robe, Jesus taking the children into His arms and blessing them. One of my favorites was about Christ calming a tumultuous storm on the Sea of Galilee with the words, "Peace, be still" (Mark 4:39).

But with the pain thundering in my head, I wondered: *Where is there any peace for me, now?* Then Mrs. Boak, the minister's wife, whom I adored, sat down beside me. "Are you okay?" she asked.

"No," I whispered. "I see flashing lights, and my head hurts." At last, I had told someone.

"You're having a migraine," Mrs. Boak said. "I know. I get them too." And the agony she described matched mine almost exactly.

I know. I get them too. My suffering had a name—a migraine—and someone else knew what it was like! When my mother took me for a checkup a month later I told the doctor about what I had been going through. "Classic migraine," he said. He wrote a prescription for tiny green pills I was to put under my tongue the moment I sensed an attack was starting.

I went on with my life, and the headaches not only tagged along, they hammered. Sometimes they struck every few weeks, sometimes months went by between attacks. It was hard to tell if the pills helped. In college I had an episode so severe that I couldn't stop vomiting, and my roommates half-carried me to the infirmary, where the doctor gave me an injection to calm my system.

After graduating from college, I moved to New York City in 1964, where I got a job at a national weekly magazine. If a migraine hit at deadline time, I tried to carry on and fight my way through—but eventually the pain forced me to go home.

I read extensively on the subject. There were all kinds of theories. Migraines came from anticipating a stressful situation or from the letdown when the stress was over, from hormones run amok or a genetic predisposition. From too much sleep, or not enough. From cheeses or nuts or chocolate or red wine. From changes in the weather. From everything from perfectionism to sloth to anger.

Editing a medical piece, I found out about a new headache clinic at a Manhattan hospital and made an appointment. Specialists took X-rays and an EEG. The diagnosis? Classic migraine. Once again I was given pills, but while they dulled the pain, they also seemed to induce a stupor that dragged on longer than the headache.

By my late thirties, migraines seemed an inextricable part of my life. One day when a colleague knocked on my closed door at lunchtime and found me with a heating pad clutched to my head, she told me about a therapist she was seeing. "I don't have migraines," she said, "but my therapist has helped me with other problems I've had."

I was ready to try anything. When I went to the therapist's office, she showed me to a cozy rocker and gave me a mug of herbal tea. Feeling comfortable, I talked to her frankly. About how I had felt as a young girl when the headaches started, about the ensuing shame that had become part of the blinding pain. During the following months, our conversations covered many things and many years in my life. "What kinds of stories meant a lot to you when you were a child?" my therapist asked.

"The stories in the Bible," I said, surprising myself, "especially the ones about Jesus. When the sick woman in the crowd touched His robe and was healed. What He said at the Last Supper. When the disciples were terrified they were going to drown, and Jesus stretched out His hand and calmed the waters."

My therapist nodded. "Think about what they mean to you and how they affect your life today," she urged. The tight tangle of emotions inside me seemed to loosen a bit.

Gradually, words and images from those Bible stories came floating back to me, often when I least expected them. My prayers took on a clearer focus: *Holy Spirit, help me to understand what is happening— when my head throbs, when my mind races with anxious thoughts, when my emotions overwhelm me, when I feel adrift in panic and pain.*

In a bookstore, I came upon a volume by Oliver Sacks, MD, the noted neurologist and author. In *Migraine: Understanding a Common*

Disorder Dr. Sacks tells of his many years studying "what is so often a dark and secret world." After discussing a number of real case histories, he talks about how migraines should not be considered "the enemy," but an integral part of each patient's makeup.

He likens the attacks to storms in the nervous system that occur after "the slow gathering of forces and tensions." Dr. Sacks observed that when his patients fought the attacks and tried frantically to halt them, the headaches were more intense and lasted longer. On the other hand, if a patient adopted an attitude of "quietism, not aggression" and rode out the full fury of the storm, the episodes were over more quickly.

"It is neither a technique nor a 'treatment' which the physician finally gives," writes Dr. Sacks. "What finally must be given is understanding—and courage: an attitude that is life-affirming in face of disease."

For the first time I began to think of my migraines not as predatory attackers to be fought off, but as a part of my identity. The next time a headache struck and I collapsed in bed, instead of tightening myself against the agony, I took a deep breath and let myself slide into it. As the pain beat on, the notion came to me: "I'm in a horrific storm. But all storms end eventually." I would take courage and see this one through.

I allowed myself to have the headache. Often I had the impression I was on a boat tossed about by waters so turbulent I feared for my life. Once, I imagined myself on the Sea of Galilee, with Jesus and His disciples, battered by angry waves. "Master," the disciples wailed, "save us, for we will surely perish." And Jesus rose from His sleep, raised His hand to the storm, and uttered three timeless words: "Peace, be still."

At once, an indescribable calm swept over me. The fear receded, my muscles relaxed, the thundering pain subsided. For a few precious moments I was in the eye of the storm. It was quiet, and I was safe.

Within seconds the pain returned. But that fragment of calm was enough to begin the healing. On some deep, unfathomable level I knew there was hope.

During the years that followed, other stories from my past came back as I lay suffering from a migraine. I heard in my mind the words of Christ at the Last Supper: *Let not your heart be troubled...I will not leave you comfortless.* Once, I actually lifted my hand like the sick woman who had touched Christ's robe, and I felt strengthened by the symbolic connection. Each time a story came to me while I was having a migraine, the tension gradually diminished and the pain lost its power—at first for moments, then for minutes, then longer.

By the mid-1980s I was working at *Guideposts.* One day, as I was reading page proofs on deadline, the lines suddenly writhed into swirls of light. Within the hour I was racked with that old, familiar pain. I went into the bathroom and lay down in the large stall intended to accommodate a wheelchair.

Curled in the far corner where no one could see me, my head pressed against the cool tiles, I took deep, slow breaths and repeated the words that had calmed me before: "Peace, be still." As the pain lessened, it occurred to me: *Here I am, a grown-up, huddled in a bathroom stall.* Instead of making me feel ashamed and embarrassed, it struck me as endearingly wacky. I started to laugh. I heard the voices of colleagues—friends—in the hall, and I felt a flood of affection for them. And with that came the realization that my relationship with my migraines was changing. For years, the headaches had held me in a joyless, tyrannical grip, solid as a rock; now their hold was loosening, allowing in the healing balm of humor and love.

My migraines continued, but each time their presence was less intense and controlling. Today, they've been reduced to an occasional display of sparkling lights and some pain that's annoying but not debilitating (I don't take anything stronger than aspirin, and I haven't collapsed on the floor of the ladies' room again).

Looking back, I know it's strange to call these episodes a friend. And yet I do. I think of the migraines with respectful fondness. The pain and disorientation were awful, but they took me on a journey that was unexpectedly rewarding. And the understanding brought by the migraines will never leave me. In the eye of the most ferocious storm, peace can be found.

28.

Patchwork Reunion
by Jill Wolpert

I SAT ON THE SOFA, COFFEE IN HAND, AND FLIPPED ON THE MORNING NEWS. ANYTHING TO DISTRACT MYSELF FROM THE GNAWING WORRY, OR MAYBE IT WAS SHEER DISBELIEF. WHAT ON EARTH WAS I THINKING? A FEW DAYS EARLIER I'D IMPULSIVELY OFFERED TO FLY ALL THE WAY ACROSS THE COUNTRY TO FLORIDA FOR MY DAD'S EIGHTIETH BIRTHDAY. SURE, EIGHTY WAS A MILESTONE, BUT MY DAD AND I DIDN'T EVEN LIKE EACH OTHER. I HADN'T SEEN HIM IN YEARS. WE HADN'T HAD A HEART-TO-HEART SINCE—WELL, HAD WE EVER HAD A HEART-TO-HEART?

Actually, I knew exactly why I'd offered to fly to Florida. Same old Jill, hoping this time I'd manage to please him. I was fifty-two years old, for heaven's sake! I had a husband and two grown kids of my own. Yet it was as if I'd never left that little house in Bay Shore, New York, where every evening Dad came home grumpy and exhausted from the auto-body shop and I made sure to stay out of his way. I couldn't honestly say whether he loved me. Every so often I tried some extravagant gesture, only to fail. This time I'd made arrangements to fly to Daytona Beach and surprise him with a fancy dinner out with my mother, my uncle, and his wife. Not only had I set myself up for failure, now I was on the hook for a gift! What do you get the man who never wanted anything from you in the first place?

I thought back bitterly over the years. All my life the word *family* meant one thing: stress. When I was very little Dad went into business for himself, opening the auto-body shop. When I was five the shop nearly went bankrupt. We lost our house and moved in with Mom's parents. Dad worked like crazy to bring the business back and Mom just about went crazy too. She didn't get along with her mother and there we were, all piled on top of one another. My older sister rebelled and spent all her time with her friends. I was the shy one. I holed up in whatever quiet room I could find and played a little chord organ that we had. Then I got into studying grasshoppers and butterflies. I made a net out of one of Mom's old stockings and started a collection. The beauty of the butterflies comforted me.

The constant refrain of my childhood was Mom warning us, "Don't bother your father." He wasn't tall but he was built like a football player and, boy, did he have a temper! Any time I was bad, his thick hand drew back to spank me. When he talked to me it was mostly to correct me. Right after I went off to college, he and Mom sold their house (the body shop eventually made money and we moved out of my grandparents') and decamped to Florida. It was like they couldn't wait to be done as parents. The final break came when I was twenty-five and pregnant with our son. We'd had a daughter two years before and, just as I'd expected, Mom and Dad didn't think much of my parenting. "You're too permissive," Mom would chide. One day on a visit I dared to disagree and Dad confronted me. "Don't you ever disrespect your mother like that!" he thundered. Shaken, I walked out, vowing never to speak to them again.

The coffee had grown cold. I swirled it around in the cup and sighed. What was I going to do? I'd already bought the plane ticket. I needed a gift. But what?

Go get the quilt. The voice spoke calmly and clearly. Startled, I looked around. The morning news hosts chatted away. California sun shone through the window—we were living in San Jose at the time, close to my husband's work. Suddenly I remembered. Ages ago, in yet another ill-advised attempt at a peace offering, I'd begun sewing a quilt for Dad. I loved quilting and all things crafty. I'd set the quilt aside pretty quickly. He wouldn't appreciate it anyway, I'd told myself. "Do I even still have it?" I wondered out loud now.

I got up and walked to the bedroom. Deep in the closet were my plastic quilt-storage bins. I rifled through one. My breath caught. There, near the bottom, were several partial sections of quilt. I pulled them out and ran my fingers over them. Was this what the voice meant?

Well, I didn't have any better ideas. What if it was God nudging me to make this quilt? I gathered the pieces and studied them. Gradually it came back to me. I'd decided to make this quilt using a repeating pattern of squares and triangles that ends up looking like rows of open monkey wrenches. Perfect for a mechanic, right?

How else could I personalize it? I looked online for embroidery patterns and quickly found one called Mourning Cloak. A butterfly. Mourning cloaks—*Nymphalis antiopa*—were the first species I ever collected. They were beautiful—mahogany wings bordered with bright blue dots and a yellow stripe. Suddenly my heart leaped with a memory. I'd brought a mourning cloak caterpillar home and raised it until it turned into a butterfly. That day, totally unexpectedly, Dad took me to meet Augie Schmitt, a professional butterfly collector in a nearby town. I'd ended up working in Augie's shop. He'd taught me everything I knew about insects. I always considered his shop a refuge from home. And yet—it had been Dad who brought me there!

I found another butterfly pattern, Tiger Swallowtail. Another memory engulfed me. I was twelve, at home one humid summer day. Dad called from the shop. "Get down here," he rumbled. I pedaled over in terror on my bike, certain I was going to catch it for something. "Look in my office," Dad said when I arrived. There, inside a jar on his desk, was a gorgeous tiger swallowtail, a black-and-yellow beauty every butterfly collector yearns for. "I found it trapped in a customer's car," Dad said gruffly. "Thought you might like it."

I stitched butterflies onto the quilt—mourning cloak, tiger swallowtail, *Papilio ulysses* from Australia. My childhood bedroom had been lined with so many lovely butterflies. I'd taken all that beauty with me when I left home. Now I could give some of it back.

I embroidered a bee because once, when I was away at college, Dad had actually added a few words in his own handwriting to a letter Mom sent. "Daddy says BEHAVE!" he wrote. That was a joke. Anytime my sister and I left the house he always barked, "Behave!" I didn't need to add "–have" to the bee. He'd get it.

Finally it was time to choose the quilt's backing. I drove to the fabric store praying I'd find the right thing. As soon as I saw a big bolt of cotton printed with a sheet-music pattern I stopped, remembering the one thing I'd been able to do to make Dad happy. As he flopped into his chair exhausted from work, I'd sit at my organ and play for him. He never said anything but I knew he liked it. He'd have told me to stop otherwise. I pictured his thickset body, his big, grease-stained hands—and I felt an overwhelming rush of love. *Oh, Daddy!* I wanted to cry. *You did love me. You just never knew how to say it.*

I went home and finished the quilt, sewing the last stitch the day before my flight. My uncle and I had planned the visit as a total surprise. I arrived in Daytona, drove to my parents' house, and parked outside. I called them on my cell phone to make them think I was still in California, then walked to the front door and knocked. They practically fell over when they saw me! "I'm taking you out for dinner," I said. At the restaurant all I could think about was the quilt. We returned to their house. The big moment had arrived. I could hardly breathe.

"Happy birthday, Daddy," I said, bringing out the quilt.

Dad didn't say a word. Was he surprised? Indifferent? I put the quilt in his calloused hands. He felt the fabric. He peered at the design. I told him what everything meant, how God had led me to each part of the design meant perfectly for him. "Remember the time…?" I kept saying. All the while, a smile slowly spread across his face, as if a lifetime were spooling through his mind. He held the quilt close and whispered, "This is mine." He looked at me a long time, tears trickling down his cheeks. In his same old gruff voice he murmured, "I love you, baby. Thank you."

I wiped away my own tears. "I love you too, Daddy."

The funny thing is, Daddy and I never had to come out and say, "I forgive you." The quilt did that for us, reminding us both of the love that had always been there between us. I don't dwell on the lost years or ask what could have been. Instead, Daddy and I talk all the time. I always pour myself a cup of coffee before I call him and I sit on the sofa, making believe we're right next to each other. There's so much to say. A lifetime of love to catch up on. I suppose forgiveness is a little like a butterfly. Even when it seems impossible, as lifeless as a dry brown chrysalis, that's when it's preparing to burst forth in new and beautiful life.

29.

"My Boat Is So Small"
by Patrick Quesnel

MY CAREFUL PREPARATION WAS PAYING OFF. MY DISCIPLINED BODY AND MIND HAD CARRIED ME, ALONE, ACROSS TWO THOUSAND MILES OF OPEN SEA AS I ROWED MY DORY, THE TWENTY-TWO-FOOT *HAWAIIKI*, TOWARD HONOLULU. I HAD LEFT THE COAST OF WASHINGTON ON JUNE 18. NOW IT WAS THE NIGHT OF NEW YEAR'S EVE. HAWAII LAY NINE HUNDRED MILES AWAY.

A strange way, certainly, to spend New Year's Eve, alone in the vastness of the Pacific. Behind me were almost two hundred days and nights; days of calm when the sun blazed down on the great, glassy rollers and nights of storm when the *Ki* swung like a frenzied cork at the end of the long line attached to the sea anchor that kept her bow pointing into the wind and waves. But I was content. More than two-thirds of my voyage lay behind me now.

I was dozing, the sea anchor holding the dory steady, when suddenly I was roused by a gigantic wave, a freakish monster that came in at a crazy angle, hurling tons of water over the *Ki* and capsizing her. I was tossed from the boat, but by hanging on to an oar as it floated past, I was eventually able to make it back to the *Ki*, right her, and start pumping. I kept working the bilge pump through the night.

When daylight came, I could see, to my horror, that most of my food and supplies had been lost or ruined. The canvas storm top, which protected the craft from the elements and fended the ocean's stormy waters from the otherwise open boat, had been ripped to pieces by the force of the wave. I was so afraid that one more freak wave might again capsize the wallowing dory that I pumped almost constantly for nearly two days.

On January 3, exhausted from pumping and facing starvation, I reluctantly put out an SOS on *Ki*'s waterproof radio. Then I wrapped myself in the torn storm top and sat down on the floorboards and cried. All my hopes and dreams were drifting away, like a rubber sponge, out to sea.

Ever since I was a kid growing up on Puget Sound, I had wanted to find adventure at sea. One day when I was ten, I read about two Scandinavian sailors, Harbo and Samuelson, who in 1896 rowed across the North Atlantic, long before anyone else had attempted such a feat. I began to dream of doing something like that.

Too restless to study, I had dropped out of college after a year. I worked at a number of jobs, but wasn't happy with any of them. I wanted to do something that had a challenge to it, something that I could do on my own.

An idea formed in my head one day when I was visiting my parents, looking at some of my boyhood photographs. Scenes of Harbo and Samuelson, rowing heroically against the Atlantic's icy swells, came back to mind.

"What would you say," I asked Mother and Dad, "if I said I wanted to row across the Pacific?"

Though they expressed concern, they offered no strong objections. They knew that if I decided to try it, I would go about it methodically, leaving nothing to chance.

So that night the thought kept running through my head. It was both a question and an answer: *Row a boat to Hawaii? Why?*

No one has ever done it. I need to prove myself, that's why.

But all that had happened two years earlier. Now, after a year of intense preparation and six months of striving alone against the sea, I'd failed.

The Coast Guard cutter *Wachusett* had just finished a tour of duty near Hawaii and was heading back home to Seattle when it picked up my SOS. After several hours of searching, while I lay huddled helplessly on the floor of *Ki*, they picked me up, and I began the long, sad journey home.

Why, I kept asking myself, had I failed? What more should I have done? What mistakes had I made?

When I got home, Mother and Dad tried to comfort me. I stored the dory and took a job as a salmon fisherman. I loved the work, but the sight and feel of the sea kept calling back the memory of my failure. I kept thinking that if I worked harder to prepare myself psychologically and physically, if I took better equipment, I just might make it on a second try.

This time I would take five ash oars, the strongest I could find from among 250 models, tested by my standing on them. I would take three plastic sextants, and a special canvas sea anchor with a 175-foot line. I decided the sea anchor I'd used was partly responsible for *Ki*'s being swamped before.

I knew how important food was. When I felt lonely or depressed at sea, I would eat. I had found that morale and meals went hand in hand. I would take different kinds of tinned meat and fish, canned and dried fruit, as many interesting canned foods as I could find. I knew that if I got tired of my food, I'd get tired, period, and be more apt to make mistakes—which I was determined not to do this time.

I would take antibiotics to help heal the saltwater sores I knew I would get, and the boils that would form from sitting and rowing so much. And I would take petroleum jelly to spread each day on my hands, and on the oarlocks too.

I would take along things to read—six novels and the New Testament, including the Psalms. As I had done on the first trip, I would rest for ten minutes of each rowing hour. During those ten minutes, I would read, disciplining myself to read no further than the end of the sentence I was on when the ten minutes were up. That way, when I rowed, I would have something to think about: What was going to happen next in the novel? At night, when I'd rest after eight to ten hours of rowing, I would listen to news and music on my radio and stay in touch with the world. I would not be overcome by loneliness, for the feeling I had experienced before, alone at sea, was a kind of benevolent solitude. I'd remembered feeling far lonelier in a room full of people.

I'd also take a small metal plaque I'd found. The plaque was inscribed with the words of the traditional Cape Cod dory-man's prayer: "O Lord, have mercy! For Thy seas are so great, and my boat is so small." I decided to fasten the plaque to *Ki*'s gunwale.

And so, on July 14, 1976, with every possible preparation made, I once again launched the dory into the sea, my heart pounding with excitement.

My plan was to row south, along the West Coast, then swing west, aided by the Baja currents, toward Hawaii.

The voyage was going as smoothly as the stroke of my oars as I left the coast of Washington behind. My confidence was growing with every hour. Then suddenly, the Pacific's tranquil mood changed.

Off Cape Blanco, at the lower end of the Oregon coast, a vicious gale came howling in from the northwest, blowing rain and saltwater spray in violent winds. My efforts to row in such a storm were completely futile. Visions of another capsizing flashed in my mind as I hung on for my life under the dory's storm top.

All through the night and the next day, the gale raged. On the third day, the storm seemed to gain force; icy breakers crashed against the dory so hard I feared they would split her hull. My whole body shivered in the wet, penetrating cold. I began to notice how much the dory's cockpit resembled a coffin; I felt defeated, doomed, and totally alone.

Then, as my eyes swept the boat, I noticed that little plaque. I moved my head closer to it and read the words: "O Lord, have mercy! For Thy seas are so great, and my boat is so small." For the first time, I understood the cry of helplessness in those simple words. They expressed exactly what I was feeling.

Since I had not thanked God when things were going well, I had dreaded what I felt was the hypocrisy of praying when I needed help. I didn't like those "gimme" prayers. But the words seemed to flow out of me now. I read them again, out loud: "O Lord, have mercy!" Then I shouted them: "O Lord, have mercy!"

Thereafter, at fifteen-minute intervals, I repeated that sailor's plea to the Master of ocean, earth, and skies. Each time, I could feel an effect on my tormented mind and body. I knew that under such menacing conditions, a man's mind could give way, but somehow I felt reassured.

On the morning of the sixth day, the storm lifted. The dory, still held by the sea anchor, rocked gently in the even swells. Weak with hunger, I wriggled from under the sodden storm top to see sunshine and clear blue sky for the first time in a week. My whole being soared like a gull, and I felt more grateful than I could ever remember. I knew that I hadn't deserved God's care and protection, but I realized now that no one ever earns God's love—that it's a free gift, available to all of us.

I knew now that God's seas really were so great that I could never claim I had conquered them alone. As I began to pull on *Ki*'s oars again, I wondered if life itself might be a lot like this voyage.

On I went, day after day through storm and calm, sustained by His Presence. At one point there was an eighty-day stretch when no ships sighted me. With no word, people at home began to worry. (I found this out later.) Many of them thought I was done for by then. Some of Mother and Dad's friends began avoiding them; they were afraid to mention me.

Then a group from our family's church, Chapel Hill United Presbyterian, in Gig Harbor, Washington, led by their minister, Dr. Frank Burgess, offered up a special prayer for my safety. Two days later, a Japanese fishing trawler spotted me and radioed that I was okay and on course, 110 miles from Hawaii.

On Tuesday, November 2, 1976, 111 days out of La Push, Washington, I pulled into Honolulu. By God's mercy, my boat, so small, had made it. I had crossed the Pacific.

But not alone or on my own. And the certain knowledge of that fact has brought me, like the steady stroke of *Ki*'s oars, closer and closer to God on the voyage of my life.

30.

I Thought I Was Too Young

by David Cornelius

IN MY MIND'S EYE I SEE A SMALL, SKINNY EIGHT-YEAR-OLD. THIS PERSON WAS ME; THAT IS, ME BEFORE I WAS CAUGHT IN LIFE'S HARSH REALITY. I WAS SMALL AND INNOCENT, TOO YOUNG FOR SUCH AN UGLY THING AS CANCER TO COME CREEPING INTO MY LIFE.

Tragedy came slowly at first, like a snowball tumbling down a hill, gradually gaining speed and size, threatening to become an avalanche. For a few weeks I dismissed the telltale signs. Then my arm got hit in physical education. The pain was so severe that Mom thought it was broken. We went to see the doctor, who took X-rays and explained that the minute spot on my upper left arm could mean trouble. He suggested that I be admitted to Gainesville Hospital, and we agreed. I stayed there for a day or two and was referred to Egleston Hospital in Atlanta. I was too young to really understand what was happening, but I wasn't too young to know that the snowball was growing.

The staff at Egleston found the cancer, and although they said I was lucky to have it diagnosed so quickly, I didn't feel lucky. There was a possibility, they said, that my left arm would have to go. Why me? What had I done to deserve this?

At Egleston, a nurse came and helped me to write a list of all the good things about my situation, should worse come to worst in the pending operation. Before I realized what was happening, I was feeling both happy and relieved. She helped me to discover how fortunate I was that my writing hand wouldn't be affected and that at my young age adjustments would be much easier.

Then the cards started coming. Although I found solace in each of hundreds that I received, one in particular filled me with wonder. It told me to read Psalm 6. I read the whole passage, but it was verse two that gave me comfort: "Have mercy upon me, O Lord; for I am weak: O Lord, heal me; for my bones are vexed." I had the odd sensation that the David of long ago had written this verse just for me, a small child with bone cancer who wanted to be healed and needed God's mercy.

After a chaotic week of testing, a surgeon informed me that a crucial biopsy would be done the next day during which the decision would be made as to whether or not they would immediately amputate my arm. The next morning, nervous and in a fog of sedation, I saw the operating light, its cold steel gleaming down on me before I went under.

When I came to, my heart leapt! I could feel my arm! It was still there. Then I looked over at my mother. The expression on her face revealed the hard truth. Suddenly I knew I had been wrong. My mind had tricked me with "phantom pain." My arm was gone.

That quote from Psalms flashed through my mind: "Have mercy upon me, O Lord," and I wondered why such a merciful God would let this happen.

I was lost, afraid, and struggling for something to help me cope. Mom was there. At that dark time, she was the only constant in my life. One day we walked through the hospital garden. It was spring and all the dogwoods stood against the fence in full bloom; squirrels were running around and birds were calling from the trees. Although, I admit, the garden was small and simple, my mother's words of praise brought out its beauty. She would point out something and proclaim what a wonder it was. Through her joyous eyes, I could see all of the wonders with which God had filled the garden.

That day, we made a pact to see the garden every time we visited the hospital later on for my treatments, so that I would have happy memories to combat the sad ones. It was with this promise and the warm air of spring that I returned home. Somehow I felt that I had avoided the avalanche.

When I got back to school, to my great surprise and relief, I was greeted by a warm banner that conveyed love, friendship, and caring in three simple words: "Welcome Back, David." Only then did I realize that I had been afraid that these people would not be able to accept me. I was overjoyed to find them welcoming me back with open arms. For the first time in my life, I realized that God really was merciful. I knew He cared about me and I was filled with hope.

Unfortunately, my hospital career wasn't quite over. I still had to go through chemotherapy. Silent torture is the only description I can think of for those treatments. At first it was the drawing of my blood that got to me. No kid likes needles, but after a while I was proud of the fact that I could take it. Then I was given shots that surged through my body killing unwary cancer cells. Regrettably, some innocent-bystander cells also had to bite the dust. The result was that, soon after the shots, I became ill and ended up spending the weekend in bed. I felt like somebody had started rolling snowballs down the mountain again.

Then I was told that one of the shots would kill my poor innocent hair cells. But I was too young to lose my hair—much too young to be dealt this insult. My hope flew out the window and for a time I hated this unmerciful world. I realized that no matter how brave and durable I made myself, that snowball was speeding down the mountain and I was right in its path. I almost gave up and let it roll over me.

I thank God Mom was there. On all our visits to the hospital, she never gave up. It must have been hard on her, but again she helped me turn to the garden as a refuge. No matter how depressed I got, she made me follow the progression of that beautiful spot through the year until spring came again and exploded with what seemed an amazing vigor. She had me convinced that nature was doing its best to uplift my spirits. It worked!

We stopped entering through the cold front doors of the hospital and started slipping past the small gate into the garden and in through the back doors. My life seemed to have leveled into a routine I could handle. Although the snowball was still there, it had not rolled over me; I felt myself healing.

Then, slowly, a strange desire welled up inside me. When I reflected on my life previous to the operation, all I could find was an ordinary boy living an ordinary life—no great accomplishments and no great downfalls. I saw my life now as better, and I decided against staying just level. My grades got better; I joined the band and discovered writing. I found that after going through the operation and chemotherapy, and dealing with my hair loss, I had gained a new self. I started actively living my life—trying to make the best of each and every day.

Today, I am what I am, molded by past experiences. Strangely enough, I like the way I've turned out and I'm happy to be alive. Thankfully, I have learned that although I can't always stop a snowball from creating an avalanche, I can use the ball to build the most beautiful snowman you have ever seen.

The Reluctant Sunday-School Teacher

by Louis A. Hill

OUR PASTOR COLLARED ME BEFORE CHURCH. "LOUIS," HE SAID, "I NEED YOU TO SUBSTITUTE TEACH A MIDDLE-AGERS' SUNDAY-SCHOOL CLASS FOR SIX WEEKS." SCARED, I MUMBLED EXCUSES.

"Please," he countered urgently, "I know you can do it. You teach college engineering students."

"But that's steel and concrete," I protested, "subjects I know cold. I'd feel like a fool standing in front of a class that knows the Bible much better than—"

"Dare to stretch!" he said. It was a clear challenge.

I was terrified. I glanced down at the Sunday-school quarterly the pastor had thrust into my hand. *Well*, I thought, *it's only for six weeks, and he's obviously desperate.*

That Sunday I felt so intimidated by my class of Bible quoters that I sometimes stammered. Yet nobody quit. In fact, in the next Sundays a few more people began to attend. When the regular teacher didn't return, I reluctantly agreed to stay on for a while.

I'd been teaching the class for three months when the pastor announced he was moving to a new church. It could take up to a year for a pulpit committee to select a new minister. That presented me with a problem I really couldn't handle: When emergencies came up in the lives of class members, they looked to me, their Sunday-school teacher, for counsel. Me, an engineer!

"I can't do that!" I told the Sunday-school superintendent. "Teaching is one thing, but I don't know the first thing about counseling."

"Don't leave now," he pleaded. "Not when you're needed the most. Isn't your wife a nurse?" I nodded. "Take her with you. She'll know what to say."

I felt too guilty to quit, and the superintendent proved to be right. Jeanne got us through a couple's anguish over a runaway teenage son, the death of a class member's beloved aunt, and another member's triple bypass surgery.

Then one night our three-year-old, Dixon, was sick with a bad ear infection. His fever was high; Jeanne was sponging him with alcohol when the phone rang near midnight.

It was the woman who'd had the triple bypass. She was gasping for breath. She'd just received word that her father had committed suicide. "Louis," she sobbed, "I just have to talk and pray with someone. Can you meet me at the church?"

"Of course," I said, though I already felt fear standing my neck hair on end. Jeanne couldn't leave Dixon. *What am I going to say that could possibly help?* I thought in anguish. I picked up my Bible and went into Dixon's room to tell Jeanne the situation just as Dixon started retching.

"Sorry," Jeanne said, "Dixon needs me. Ask God to give you the right words. In the Book of Luke He promised He would."

On the way to the sanctuary I got so upset that I had to pull over. *If I say the wrong thing, I could cause a heart attack.* I turned on the dome light and opened my Bible. Shortly the words leaped out at me: "Don't be concerned about what to say...for the Holy Spirit will give you the right words even as you are standing there" (Luke 12:11–12 TLB).

When I arrived at church, the woman was getting out of her car, her shoulders sagging. I hurried to her and hugged her. "Louis, what will happen to Daddy's soul?" she asked, her voice a tortured whisper.

"Remember," I heard myself answer, "in First Chronicles, David tells us that God's mercy is very great." Then, as we went inside and knelt at the altar, I was amazed to hear myself spilling out Scripture in a comforting voice. I, who had never memorized, was reciting verses that described God's mercy. It was my voice, that much I knew, but the words were being given to me. The distraught woman was visibly calmed. I said a silent prayer of gratitude.

I never had to take Jeanne with me again. I knew I could depend on God to help me handle any emergency. And the spiritual growth I experienced during those emergencies helped me become a better teacher. After nine years, my class had grown to seventy members. I felt so confident that I applied for the position of dean of engineering at the University of Akron—and I was chosen! Teaching Sunday school had stretched my career as well.

Since then I've retired from the university, but I'm still teaching Sunday school. How could I give up something that has taught me so much?

32.

Big Trouble in Paradise
by Wanda Davis

"I'LL GO FIRST," MY FRIEND KATHY SAID. I'D ASKED KATHY TO AC-
COMPANY ME ON A CRUISE TO THE BAHAMAS. OUR CRUISE SHIP
HAD STOPPED FOR AN AFTERNOON IN FREEPORT, AND KATHY
AND I HAD JUST GOTTEN UP THE NERVE TO TRY PARASAILING
OVER THE PELICAN BAY. NOW WE WERE WAITING AT THE DOCK
FOR OUR TURNS.

"It's like being flown on a kite," a woman who'd gone before us
said. "It's a blast!" Harnessed to a sail, we'd fly high in the sky tethered
securely to a speedboat by a six-hundred-foot towrope. The crew on
the dock assured us that it was absolutely safe, scores of tourists like
us had done it every day for sixteen years. And this day of all days
looked perfect—clear blue sky, soft tropical breeze, only the slightest
chop in the water.

I'm a careful person, never one to take risks. I like to feel in control.
But now that I'd worked up my courage, I was determined to try parasailing. Still, I watched nervously as Kathy pulled on her life vest and
was strapped into the parachute's harness. The speedboat roared to
life and Kathy was lifted into the air, borne by the breeze.

I could see the look of exhilaration on Kathy's face. The view must be incredible, I marveled. The boat pulled her around the bay for five minutes, finally swinging around to the dock in front of the Grand Bahama Beach Hotel. Two guys grabbed the towrope and guided it under a hook. Still pulling, the boat motored away from the dock, lowering Kathy toward the crews' outstretched hands. She landed with a hop and a whoop, grinning from ear to ear. It looked so fun. *Relax and enjoy this*, I told myself. *You're here to have a good time.*

My heart raced as I was strapped into a life jacket, then clipped into the fabric harness attached to the parachute. *Okay, Lord*, I asked silently, *You wouldn't let me do anything foolish, right?* The boat eased forward until the towline was taut, the guys on the dock held the parachute up, and *whoosh*, I was off.

I shut my eyes as the towrope was let out farther, taking me higher and higher into the sky. As the warm tropical air rushed against my face, I got enough courage to open my eyes and look down. I gazed at the shimmering water below. I could see clear to the bottom. *Thank You, Lord, for letting me see the island in such a beautiful way.* At last I relaxed. I was completely at the mercy of the wind—and it felt wonderful, so wonderful to let go of my fear.

Then, well out over the bay, a strong gust abruptly pulled the parachute. My harness jerked. Another gust and a jolt. Was this supposed to happen? I glanced toward the horizon. Dark, angry clouds boiled up out of nowhere, rolling in my direction—fast. The sun disappeared and the breeze became chill. Below me the water had turned frothy with whitecaps. *God, get me down*, I thought, *and I'll never try this again!*

The boat turned sharply and started back to the dock. The wind knocked me from side to side. My stomach churned. *Hurry*, I urged. At last we approached the dock and the crew members stood ready to grab my towrope.

The crew had just hooked the rope to the pole on the dock when—*whaap!* A powerful updraft hit the parasail, the speedboat spun around, almost capsizing. The crew unhooked the rope from the pole and, as I swung terrified in the darkening sky, shouted frantically for help. They couldn't reach my towrope and the boat didn't have the power to fight the wind and waves.

Another speedboat roared toward us. The two boats were lashed together. The drivers revved their motors and with their combined power pulled on the towrope, trying to get me close enough to the dock so the crew could hook the rope. Then the wind hit gale force, hurtling the two boats toward shore, sweeping them out of the water and onto the beach.

"Help!" I shouted. Palm trees bent toward the ground under the force of the wind. On the beach, people stopped to stare and point at me, others came running from the hotel below. A woman screamed. I clung to the straps above me. I felt a sickening snap. The towrope broke! My parasail shot straight up. Up, up, up, over two hundred feet in a matter of seconds.

People scrambled to catch the end of the rope, but it was far over their heads, and I was going too fast. I sailed over the five-story Grand Bahama Beach Hotel, the rope dragging behind me, like the leash of an errant dog.

A man working on the hotel roof gaped at me as I shot by, a look of astonishment frozen on his face. The parasail dropped and the rope dragged across a construction area hundreds of feet below. Still the parasail zoomed on, with me dangling helplessly beneath it.

The rope end was bouncing along a four-lane highway. Ahead of me was the Port Lucaya Marketplace, a row of flat buildings we'd visited earlier that day. Suddenly I was dropping. *I'm going to hit them!* I squeezed my eyes shut and kept saying, "God, please save me" over and over. Just as suddenly the wind lifted the parachute, barely missing the last building in the complex.

Even though I'd been in the sky for only minutes, it seemed like hours. My legs were numb from hanging in the harness. My left arm had been jerked so hard I couldn't move it. Emergency sirens wailed below. I could see ambulances darting around traffic as they sped after me. Crowds of people were running along too, tiny frantic figures.

I was being blown closer and closer to the ocean. What would happen if I was blown out to sea? They'd never find me. *God, You created the wind and the waves. Please control this parasail.* Then I grasped what I was saying. *You created the wind.* God was in the wind.

It was in His power to turn this gale into a gentle breeze that would drop me safely to the ground. Just as I felt completely at the mercy of the wind, it was necessary to give myself over completely to the mercy of God. I had to relax and let Him take control, to let go and let God. *Lord, I'm in Your hands. I trust You to carry me where You want me to go.*

I looked down and saw a sliver of water ahead of me. "There!" I shouted out loud. "God, please drop me there." At that moment the wind gave a final bellow, then calmed. I was coming down fast, headed right for what seemed to be a canal. In the next instant, the wind died completely and the parasail floated downward like a petal. Giving a final flutter, it gently collapsed into the water about ten feet from the seawall.

I floundered to free myself from the sinking sail. Had I gotten this far only to drown? *Relax*, I reminded myself. *Remember Who's in control.*

A man came running. "Unhook your life jacket from the parasail!" he shouted. I managed to hold my left arm across the vest, pushing it down, and with my other hand squeezed the clasps. As the water rose around me, the clasps clicked open and I was free.

Moments later rescue workers pulled me out of the canal. As they carried me toward an ambulance, someone asked me where I was, to see if I still had my senses. "What time is it?" he then asked, tapping his watch. "Honey," I said, "I'm over forty. I can't see that dial without my glasses." He grinned. "She's got a broken arm but she's okay!" The crowd who'd been following me cheered.

A man showed me his red and blistered palms. "Rope burns," he explained. "I tried to catch your rope when you passed over." Everyone seemed amazed that I wasn't dead.

"I want you to know that you just witnessed a miracle," I said.

A lady touched my arm. "You are mightily blessed," she said with an island lilt that made me laugh with relief and joy.

At the hotel the next day, people saw my arm in a sling and kept asking if I was "the parasailing lady." Others filled me in on what had happened on the ground while I was in the air. The broken towrope had been dragged across a moving taxi, startling the driver off the road—fortunately no one was hurt. A construction worker said the debris I'd flown over had been set with dynamite, and he was surprised they hadn't been blasting. Later, I talked to the parasailing crew, who said that in all their years on the island, they'd never seen the weather change so abruptly.

I shuddered with fear. If an accident like this could happen out of the blue, what other uncontrollable event might next befall me? Then I reminded myself Who it was that made the wind and the waves. And that night on the ship as I drifted to sleep, lulled by the faraway sound of a gentle breeze, I relaxed, knowing that no matter what happened, I was in God's hands.

33.

Rheumy Toad

by Jean Bell Mosley

I HAVE LIVED WITH RHEUMY TOAD FOR MORE THAN TWO YEARS. DOCTORS USE ANOTHER TERM FOR HIM—RHEUMATOID ARTHRITIS. BUT I LIKE THE NAME I'VE GIVEN HIM BETTER. AND I'VE DECIDED I'M NOT GOING TO LET THIS BUG-EYED, SAD-FACED, WARTY OLD AMPHIBIAN GET ME DOWN.

When I was first diagnosed, I failed to see anything funny. My body stiffened and twisted. My shoulders hurt, my hips and knees balked at moving. In my distress, both physical and emotional, it occurred to me to give my illness a name. That's how Rheumy Toad was born.

On a day when Toady is very active, he makes it hard for me to use my pen and notebook. Nonetheless I have managed to draw pictures of him. Most of them make me laugh, which chases Toady away for a spell.

I have come to tolerate Rheumy and even to accept him. After all, he is my toad, different from anyone else's. He gives me something to pit my brains and strength against, and he intensifies my focus on the issues that are truly worthwhile. It's his persistence that sends me to the Scriptures to "restoreth my soul," to be assured by the words of Christ that whatever happens "I will not leave you comfortless."

Toady is very determined. He may go away for a while, but inevitably he returns. He could be called The Comeback Toad. Pen and notebook are fine palliatives against the debilitating pain of body and spirit. On difficult days, I write messages to Rheumy:

"Toady, you have a one-track mind, set on making my limbs ache and crippling my body. But my mind is multifaceted. I can send it at will to wander through green pastures, sit in fragrant gardens, or relive a laugh I shared with friends or a scene from *I Love Lucy*. While you are trying to make me wince with pain, I have memories that make me smile."

"Rheumy Toad, do you know that men and women in white coats diligently work with test tubes, new drugs, and advanced procedures to find something that will banish you forever?"

I also write to God. "Heavenly Father, I do not ask for bread, clothing, or shelter. You have given me these in abundance. I ask only that You give me increased endurance and patience to live with my pain. May the sense of humor You gave me never fail; and even though my joints ache, keep my funny bone in good working order. Let me never forget that life, glorious life, is a gift on any terms."

34.

The Light in the Courtroom

by Richard S. Whaley

WHEN I WAS A YOUNG MAN AND HAD PRACTICED LAW IN THE STATE OF SOUTH CAROLINA ONLY A SHORT TIME, I WAS SUR-PRISED ONE MORNING BY A VISIT FROM AN UNCLE OF MINE. HE WAS ONE OF THE FEW REMAINING SOUTHERNERS OF THE OLD SCHOOL; COURTESY AND PUNCTILIOUSNESS WERE THE KEY-NOTES OF HIS EVERY ACT.

"Dick," he drawled, "many years ago, your grandfather on your mother's side had a family of slaves, by the name of Holmes. Some of the Holmes boys now seem to be tied up with a bunch of bad charac-ters. There's been a murder down in the County, and the prosecutor is pressing a case against the Holmeses. It will be coming up for a trial in the next session. That Holmes family was mighty good to us Whaleys in the days of our troubles. I been kind of hoping that there is some mistake somewhere. But I know nothing about it. Somehow, I can't just stand by, and I kind of reckoned that you, knowing the law, might take over?"

I confess that in those days I was looking for better retainers. In similar cases, about all I received as a fee would be perhaps a dozen chickens or so. I was just about to find some good excuse when Uncle Ben, whose piercing eyes seemed to read my thoughts, spoke out loud to himself as if I was not present at all.

"Yes, when those Yanks cleaned us out," Uncle murmured, "the food situation became desperate. The Holmes family, down to the smallest curly head, foraged all day long, and late in the evening.

"We were about to give up after days without nourishment, with Grandma and Grandpa very feeble. The Holmeses returned, built up the kitchen fire, and soon prepared the best tasting soup and meals we had for a long, long time. I have often heard it said that the lives of the old folks were saved by that soup. Those former slaves kept us alive—and well. They provided for us a long time, till things got better."

I felt ashamed of any selfishness. All I could do was to stammer, boylike: "Then, if it hadn't been for the Holmeses, I might not be here, much less be a lawyer."

As if satisfied with my reaction, my uncle Ben stood up and, with a most courteous bow, shook my hand without further word and left me to come to my own decision.

I was soon doing nothing else but investigating all the facts of the murder case and the incidents in the lives of the Holmes boys. I also got to know almost every twig in the neighborhood of the crime. I watched the mannerism of the suspected boys, but while I felt convinced of their innocence, I could find no way to prove it.

There were simply too many circumstances that unexplained, pointed to their guilt. The very simplemindedness of the boys, which convinced me of their honesty, was a weakness against them. When the trial started, I was sick at heart over my lack of a good case.

Day after day, the prosecutor fitted in his condemning evidence like pieces of a mosaic. Like the keystone of an arch, he produced as his main witness a detective who had a natural clarity of expression, and a highly impressive delivery. Word after word beat into the minds of the jury, who seemed almost hypnotized.

In the late afternoon, the prosecutor was about to conclude his case when the court ordered an adjournment to the next day. When the courtroom emptied, I sank down in my chair exhausted, beaten.

I seemed to breathe rather than speak, "Oh, God, do not allow an injustice to happen to these boys. Let Your Holy Spirit pour wisdom and strength through me. We are lost without Your help."

I sat a long while lost in a sense of prayer—of growing assurance of God's mercy and justice. I was roused by the sound of footsteps in the big empty chamber and looked up.

There stood a complete stranger. He approached me and said, "Did you know, son, a man can get a detective certificate and badge for two dollars? See, here is the Savannah newspaper advertisement where it says so."

"Well, what of it?" I muttered wearily. The stranger handed me the paper, gave an odd smile and nod, and sauntered off again without an answer. I stared at the printed words and my mind began to click. I began to pace around the room in mounting excitement. Was prayer answered that quickly?

For a scene had flashed through my mind—a scene that had occurred several days ago in the corridor. It was such an insignificant incident that it seemed amazing that I remembered it at all. A certain man had approached the prosecutor's star witness, the detective, and said in a rather ribald manner: "Jim, when are you going to pay me that two bucks you borrowed?"

The next day in court this detective was in the witness stand when the judge tersely announced to me: "Your cross-examination." His manner plainly indicated that he figured I had a hopeless case.

I stood up with a prayer—and the Savannah newspaper in my hand. Then to everyone's amazement I asked the detective, "Did you borrow two dollars a while back from Mr. Jones? I heard him ask you the other day when you were going to pay."

The detective was caught off guard. He reddened and stammered. The prosecutor leaped to his feet and objected. The jury stared at me with looks of both pity and bafflement.

"Of course, in so important a case as this you are prepared to submit your certificate entitling you to act as a detective," I insisted calmly.

There was no mistaking the red-faced look on the detective's face now as he handed forth his certificate. One glance at the fancy engraved paper and its recent date was enough for me. Suddenly it seemed as if all the power in the universe was in my sinews. I produced the Savannah journal, read the "ad" to the judge and jury, and I took this fling at the thoroughly abashed detective who had tried to pass as an expert:

"And with the two dollars you borrowed from Jones, you bought this certificate and badge!"

The detective was completely discredited when he admitted it. Nothing he said thereafter had any effect on the jury. In fact, his impressive delivery was gone and he was in a hurry to get it all over with and leave all those disgusted and mocking faces in the courtroom.

The jury remained out but a few moments. Their verdict: "Not Guilty." The Holmes boys were free.

"Illuminate me with Thy Holy Spirit," said Dr. Samuel Johnson. Whenever I read this prayer I cannot help but think of that trial which was so significant in my life, not only because it paid off a family debt of saving life for life; not only because it kept two innocent men from a shameful end; and not only because it chalked up justice to African Americans in the South—but because early in my career it taught me to seek God's help and ask for His Holy Spirit to enlighten me.

All my life, I've begun my day in court with a silent earnest prayer. I would not dream of undertaking work without it.

35

My Restless Search
by Fulton Oursler

ONE APRIL MORNING WHEN I WAS A CHILD, MY NURSE LED ME TO A GRAY-STONE CHAPEL IN BALTIMORE. WELCOMING ME INSIDE, A SUNDAY-SCHOOL TEACHER AWESOMELY INFORMED ME THAT I WAS NOW IN GOD'S HOUSE.

"Whereabouts," I asked, "is God?"

"God," the lady assured me, "is everywhere."

But I wanted Him to be somewhere. That was why I refused to sit still on my little oaken chair and ran about the room during the singing of "Little Drops of Water." I peeked under the pew and in a broom closet, only to be rescued finally, breathless and dusty, from behind the pipe organ, weeping because I had not found God.

Thus my quest began, and through half a century I never entirely abandoned it. Even in childhood the reality or non-reality of the Creator seemed to me the most important matter in life; nor can I understand today how any intelligent person can think otherwise. It is the one supreme matter on which a man has to be sure, for every decision he makes hinges upon it.

In my search for truth, I explored many different fields. A study of comparative religions over a decade of years led me from Buddhism, all the way to Bahaism and Zoroastrianism. As a reporter for the *Baltimore American*, I attended many religious conferences, and covered evangelistic meetings of Billy Sunday. I even waited for specters in dark-room séances of spiritualistic mediums.

Out of all this I emerged, at the age of thirty, a self-styled agnostic. In those days I considered myself a liberal person, emancipated from superstition, although still genially loyal to ethical values—when they did not interfere too much with what I wanted to do.

Such tolerance and emancipation, and what I considered common sense and goodwill, should have brought me happiness but did not. Nor did they bring happiness to anyone I knew. Most of my friends felt as I did; none of us better or worse than the other, I suppose; all very independent and self-reliant and disdainful of the old-fashioned faith of our fathers. We all had a great deal of fun, too, but somehow our hilarities left us dispirited.

With our freedom, we should have known a high sense of contented integrity. Not one of us knew any such security. Instead we all had an inner restlessness of disappointment and discontent.

This inner sulkiness and depression had nothing to do with material success. Among my friends were many who had achieved fame and riches, or, at least, a lot of money in the bank. But no matter how much more wealth they piled up, how often their pictures were on the front page, their new possessions, their new wives—nothing was ever enough. After they got what they wanted, they didn't want it. Without avail, they haunted doctors and psychiatrists and yogis.

The world in which I lived was a world of self-pity, self-justification, alibis, envies, jealousies, greeds, fears, resentments, grudges, and hatreds. Today was never good enough, but tomorrow they hoped to be glad. I say they, but I mean we. I shall be forever grateful that in the midst of mental bleakness I found the way out. It is not easy to tell how this happened; I cannot bring myself to open old wounds to public gaze. But you may remember the true story of the illustrious refugee at Lourdes, a famous liberal writer who, with his wife, had slipped through the Nazi frontier. They were working their way southward from Germany through France. The Gestapo was after them, and capture meant the concentration camp or worse. Their hope was to cross the Spanish border and sail for the United States.

But they were stopped by Spanish officials. Bribes and entreaty alike failed; they were turned back and found a lodging in the little town in the Pyrenees called Lourdes. On his first night there the fugitive writer stood in front of the famous shrine and made a prayer, a cry from the heart.

"I do not believe in You," he said, in effect, "and I must be honest and say so. But my danger is great, and in my extremity, on the chance that You might after all be real, I ask Your help. See my wife and me safely across the barrier, and when I get to the United States I will write the story of this place for all the world to read."

Strange as it sounds, Franz Werfel and his wife got safely through, within the week. The first thing he did, once safe in our land, was to write *The Song of Bernadette*. In our day no more popular tribute to faith was ever penned than the story written by the refugee novelist. Before he died he told me that in the terror of his plight he had come to know God and thereafter had never lost the sense of His presence.

Now something akin to that happened to me. It was nothing so spectacular as a flight from Hitler's agents, but within my own modest sphere I, too, felt surrounded and in danger and afraid. My agnostic self-reliance was no longer helpful; trouble came and littered my doorstep. Not only I, but those nearest and dearest to me were in trouble, until I felt I really needed God's help. Yet even then I could not, as an intelligent man, command myself to believe or pretend to obey—for a man is a fool who tries to deceive either God or himself. The most—the best that I could manage was to admit to myself that I wished I could believe.

And that was enough!

Faith is a gift—but you can ask for it! "O Lord," prayed a man in the Bible, "I believe; help Thou mine unbelief." As he laid his situation before God, and as Werfel did, so did I. Not in Palestine, nor in the Pyrenees, but close to the fashionable parade on Fifth Avenue. On a blustery day, with dark clouds lowering, I turned suddenly into a house of God and asked for the gift of faith. And in the chapel, I took one more vital step.

"In ten minutes or less I may change my mind," I prayed. "I may scoff at all this and love error again. Pay no attention to me then. For this little time I am in my right mind and heart. This is my best. Take it and forget the rest; and, if You are really there, help me."

It was a striking omen to me that when I came out on the steps the sun had crashed through the dark skies and the lordly avenue was full of color and light.

Merely for the record, the perplexities of my problem were most remarkably and swiftly disposed of. The complication dissolved itself by the oncoming of a series of what the rationalist would call beautiful coincidences. In two weeks I no longer had a serious problem.

But for me the real knowing of God was just beginning on that day. Only incidentally is prayer asking for help. Prayer is not a slot machine, where you drop in a request and a boon comes tumbling out of the bottom. We do pray for help, but oftener we pray for help for others, and even oftener we pray our thanks for blessings already received. Above everything else, we pray daily in sheer felicity, in communion, in close contact with the Father, asking nothing whatever but the joy of knowing Him.

It is through prayer that we know there is a God, that God is there; through prayer that we know Him—as Father and friend.

Even with this new feeling of profound tranquility, nevertheless, you want to be active. Your kind instincts will no longer be satisfied with sending checks to worthy charities; you will be ashamed to buy yourself off. Such gifts to charity are necessary, but never enough. We have to do the corporal works of mercy ourselves; and, as we come to know God, the urge to serve Him personally becomes overpowering. We must feed the hungry, visit the sick, comfort the widow and orphan, clothe the naked, shelter the shelterless—under our own roof, with our own bare hands.

That is when a human being comes closest to God and knows Him best.

Isn't it strange that it should have taken me fifty years to find that simple key to the mystery? Ten thousand times in that half century, God walked with me to school, rode with me in the bus, held out a beggar's hand at the corner alley, roared at me in the very blasphemy of a reeling old sot from whom all had fled. So many times He was at my elbow, and I pushed on, unaware. Fifty years of never noticing! I have much lost time to make up for.

36

A Deeper Surrender
by John Sage

I USED TO LIVE AS IF I WERE IN TOTAL CONTROL OF MY LIFE. IF I WANTED SOMETHING, I WENT AFTER IT UNTIL I GOT IT. THAT'S HOW I BECAME AN ALL-AMERICAN TACKLE ON THE FOOTBALL TEAM AT LOUISIANA STATE UNIVERSITY. AFTER GRADUATION I WAS DRAFTED BY THE NFL, BUT I PASSED UP A PRO CAREER TO GO INTO BUSINESS FOR MYSELF IN HOUSTON, AND TO MARRY A BEAUTIFUL WOMAN NAMED FRANCES. AT JUST THIRTY-SIX YEARS OLD, IT SEEMED I'D ACCOMPLISHED IT ALL. I'D BECOME A MILLIONAIRE ENTREPRENEUR WITH A DEVOTED WIFE AND TWO FINE SONS. I SHOULD HAVE BEEN ON TOP OF THE WORLD. *SO WHY AREN'T YOU?* I WONDERED.

I didn't have the answer to that. All I knew was that something was very wrong with me. My nights were spent tossing and turning, and during the day I felt so listless I could hardly function. In less than one month I lost twenty-five pounds. *Maybe I should see a doctor.*

"I don't know what's going on," I said after he'd examined me.

"You're suffering from clinical depression, John," the doctor told me. "Most likely it's being caused by a chemical imbalance in your brain, and exacerbated by stress."

I refused to accept his diagnosis. *Look at all you've accomplished,* I told myself. *What do you have to be depressed about?*

Yet getting through the days became more torture than I could bear. Everything I'd worked for was crumbling, just like I was on the inside. I could hardly talk about it to anyone—not Frances, not even my sister Marilyn. That surprised me, because Marilyn and I were as close as could be, and I knew she wanted the best for me. I thought about asking God to help, but how could He? It was my problem to solve.

But nothing I did made it better. Finally, I decided the doctor had been right, and I found a good therapist and started taking medication. Within a year, the dark cloud lifted. I promised myself I'd never feel such pain again.

While I had been in the depths of depression, my business suffered. I struggled for eight hard years trying to put things back in order. Still, I'd been through the wringer of depression and come out all right. I would get through this too. Hadn't I proved I was strong enough to face anything?

Then came a horrible day one June. I had left work and was only a few blocks from home when my car phone rang. It was Frances. "Johnny, something horrible has happened!" she said. "Marilyn's dead! Someone killed her!"

"I'll be right there," I said, flooring the gas pedal. *My sister, dead? It can't be!* But when I got home and saw Frances's face, I knew it was true. Marilyn. We'd just had dinner together three nights earlier. She'd noticed I was feeling a little down, so before I left she'd hugged me and said, "Johnny, you're the greatest." Next to Frances, no one made me feel more loved than Marilyn.

We'd been born nineteen months apart, the fourth and fifth in a family of eight children. From the time we were toddlers, we were inseparable. Marilyn was a tomboy, tagging along behind me to build forts, climb trees, and play football. The two of us carpooled in school, and she followed me to LSU for college, where she insisted on doing my laundry for me every week. I ended up marrying her close friend Frances. I couldn't remember a time when Marilyn hadn't been a part of my life.

Nor could I bear to think about how her life had ended, especially after one detective told me, "I've investigated homicides for twenty-five years, and I've never seen anything this brutal." But I pressed him for the details. He told me Marilyn had been stabbed with at least three different knives, bludgeoned with a statue, and suffocated with a plastic bag.

Just forty-eight hours later, police arrested two nineteen-year-olds, a boy and girl, who confessed to the murder. They'd been cruising the neighborhood where Marilyn lived, looking for a car to steal, when they spotted my sister removing some clothes from her trunk. They crept into her apartment behind her and attacked her when she came down the hall. She never had a chance.

The rage and grief I felt were indescribable. I wanted nothing more than for those two to suffer the way my sister had. I fantasized about killing them. I wished I'd been there to protect Marilyn. But I hadn't been, and now she was gone. *If someone as good and loving as Marilyn can be taken from us, what point is there to life?* I wondered. Her death triggered something in me. I felt hopeless and helpless. I began sleeping less, eating less. I had panic attacks, and my stomach churned unceasingly. The symptoms were all too familiar—depression.

I was furious with myself for succumbing to it. Hadn't I been through this already? How could I fight it again? Rage overwhelmed me. I couldn't function, and ended up quitting my job. I had to file for disability, a huge blow for a proud man like me. Or the man I once had been.

The following January, I dragged myself into the bathroom after yet another sleepless night. The man in the mirror was not someone I recognized. His eyes were bloodshot, his face unshaven, his shoulders slumped. I turned away, disgusted. Marilyn's last words to me rang in my mind: "Johnny, you're the greatest." The greatest what? Failure? Lunatic? What would she think of me now?

All at once I started crying. "Just tell me what to do, God," I pleaded.

"Give it to Me, John," a voice seemed to answer.

I fell to my knees right there on the cold tile floor. "God, I can't go on like this," I prayed. "I'm letting go and trusting You to be in charge of my life."

I felt relief after saying those words, but living them was something else. First, I made the decision to go back to a therapist and back on medication. Having to admit I needed help again was an exercise in humility for me, but I couldn't go on the way I was. Within a few months I felt I was becoming my old self. But then one of Marilyn's killers went on trial.

In the courtroom, I studied the young man sitting at the defense table. Wearing a suit and tie with his hair neatly trimmed, he didn't look like the monster I knew he was. As the prosecutor played a tape of the young man's confession, I rose from my seat. In my mind's eye I could see my hands wrapping around the young man's throat, squeezing the life out of him. It would feel so good to take his life, just as he'd taken Marilyn's.

"John, stop!" shouted a voice in my head. I snapped back to reality and tried to focus on the proceedings. The prosecution had moved on to showing photos of the crime scene. I couldn't bear to look. Instead, I shut my eyes tight and prayed, *Lord, get me through this. Take away the pain, please. And let the jury hang that predator.* I knew it wasn't fair to ask such a thing, but I had to see this man pay.

It didn't take long—the trial lasted only five days. The jury took under an hour to come back with a guilty verdict, and even less time to assess the death penalty. *One down, one to go!* I thought. It was another long year until his female accomplice was found guilty and sentenced to death as well.

Finally I could move on. Yet why did I feel nothing had been resolved? I was no better off with the murderers on death row. It wouldn't bring my sister back. In a way, I'd become a prisoner too—of my own rage and depression. *How long until I get my life back?* I demanded of God. Then I thought of my promise to Him: "I'm letting go and trusting You." *If you really had given it all to Him*, I told myself, *maybe you wouldn't be feeling this way now.* My prayer in the bathroom hadn't been enough. Nor had going back to therapy and medication. I was still trying to be in control, but the only thing I was really in control of was my own misery. What God wanted from me was a deeper surrender, a full and unconditional reliance on His loving will for me.

I threw myself into my spiritual commitment in a way I never had before. I prayed daily, hourly. I joined a Bible study group, and it was there I learned what Jesus said to God in the Gospel of John: "You sent Me and have loved them even as You have loved Me." God loved me? As much as He loved His own Son? I could hardly fathom such an idea. But it was right there in black and white. Was that what I had been missing all along—God's love? He seemed to be telling me it was, and that the key to receiving that love was to let go once and for all.

So I kept on with therapy, medication, and spiritual pursuits. Gradually, things evened out. My depression lifted and I was able to go back to work. I was able to spend more time with my sons and take the whole family out for dinner and a movie. And I tried not to think about my sister's killers.

One day, four years after Marilyn's death, I got a phone call from a reporter for a national TV news magazine. "Your sister's killer has an execution date in a few months," she said. "Are you excited?"

"No," I said hesitantly, "I'm not."

"But this awful woman, you can watch her get the lethal injection. Won't it feel good?"

"No, it wouldn't feel good," I told her.

"I'm amazed you're not even angry!" the reporter snapped, hanging up abruptly.

In a way, so was I. Once, the only thing I could think about was what I wanted to do to Marilyn's killers, and it drove me to despair. Now it seemed like that was another lifetime. Sitting there with the phone in hand, I tried to resurrect the hatred I'd felt. But I couldn't do it. It struck me that somewhere during the previous year I had let go of my anger and desire for revenge and put my life—all of it—in someone else's hands. How else could I explain my reaction to that reporter's attempts to inflame me?

At that point I knew I had reached the place Marilyn would want me to be—where I could give God all my pain and He would give me the love I needed to take its place.

37.

The Woman I Called Gram

by Elizabeth D. Kelly

NEW HAMPSHIRE WAS WHERE I HAD SPENT MOST OF MY LIFE AND WHERE THINGS HAD FALLEN APART—MY MARRIAGE HAD DISSOLVED; I'D LOST MY JOB, THEN MY HOME. I HAD COME TO FLORIDA, THINKING MAYBE I COULD START OVER. BUT HERE I WAS, CAMPED OUT WITH MY KIDS AT A FRIEND'S PLACE. THE ONLY WORK I COULD FIND WAS PART-TIME. I WAS FORTY-TWO YEARS OLD AND HAD NO WAY TO SUPPORT MY FAMILY, NO HOME, NOWHERE I REALLY BELONGED. I'D MADE A MESS OF PRETTY MUCH EVERY OPPORTUNITY I'D EVER BEEN GIVEN. AND MAYBE I DIDN'T DESERVE ANOTHER CHANCE. MAYBE THERE REALLY WAS NO HOPE FOR ME.

Then Meredith called me from New Hampshire. "Elizabeth? I'm sorry to be the bearer of bad news, but your gram's in a bit of a fix." I caught my breath. Meredith was the daughter-in-law of Minerva Beal, the woman who had taken me in to her Manchester, New Hampshire, group home when I was an infant and basically raised me. She was the woman I called Gram. The one constant in my crazy life. Recently she'd had heart surgery, and I had visited her just before I left for Florida.

"Are you still looking for work?" Meredith asked. Before I could answer she said, "Because Gram's caregiver is moving away and we could really use you up here. You and your kids could live in Gram's house."

I felt like I'd been whiplashed—anxious for Gram, stunned at this sudden lifeline. "I—I need to run it by the kids first," I replied. But inside I knew.

My birth mom, unmarried when she had me, frankly admitted she couldn't care for me or my two older sisters when she dropped us off at Gram's group home, Boylston Home for Girls. Gram and her husband, Earl ("Grampy" to me), a minister, were my real parents, even after they retired from the group home seven years later and my sisters and I went to live with my father. Whenever Dad's depression got bad, he'd leave us at the Beals' house in Londonderry. Gram still lived there. That house, with its simple antique furnishings and wall hangings stitched with Scripture verses, had always been a refuge for me. Two days after Meredith phoned, my kids and I were on a plane to New Hampshire.

"Oh, Elizabeth, it's so wonderful to see you!" Gram exclaimed when I arrived. No tsk-ing at the mess I'd made of my life. No embarrassment at being taken care of. Just smiles, hugs, and kisses, especially for my son and daughter, fifteen-year-old Michael and four-year-old Siobhan. The house had four bedrooms, so there was space for all of us.

"You should sleep in your old room," Gram said to me. After settling the kids, I walked into the room. There was my twin bed with the wood headboard, the small bookshelf, and dresser. I swallowed hard to keep from crying. The old peace still inhabited this room, but I couldn't help wondering whether I'd somehow put myself beyond its reach. I'd taken so many wrong turns since those childhood days.

Memories flooded in. Grampy striding purposefully through the house, whistling some hymn. Gram playing checkers with my sisters and me, serving up vanilla ice cream made with real vanilla beans after dinner. I especially loved the way Scripture wove so effortlessly through Gram's everyday conversation. Usually kids make fun of that kind of piety, but I never did. How could I when her faith so plainly infused her whole life? She and Grampy could have let my sisters and me go the day we arrived at the group home. The other children were wards of the state receiving public assistance. Our parents were technically obligated to pay for us but never did. The home's board of directors encouraged the Beals to turn us out. Grampy refused, saying he'd quit before he did any such thing. Instead, he took on extra preaching jobs to afford our upkeep. "Love is for keeps," Gram liked to say, her voice as strong and vital as she was.

It was hard seeing her so weak now. She often used a wheelchair. I was at her side from dawn until bedtime. I cooked, cleaned, got her up, and dressed and brushed her hair. Most days she spent in an old easy chair in the living room. There we read out loud—she loved a devotional called *Daily Light*—and talked about old times. "You were such a thoughtful little girl," Gram told me. "There was lots of turmoil in your life, but whenever you were here you were such a joy."

Really? I couldn't stop thinking about all the times I'd tested the Beals' generosity. When I was twelve, my mother suddenly reemerged and took me to live with her. Three years later, I ran away. I was wild. Two years after that, dumped by an abusive husband, I called the Beals collect. "Come home," they said. It was what they always said—when I got pregnant at age twenty; when my second marriage to the father of that child crumbled many years later; even now, at yet another of my numerous dead ends. Why, I wondered, did Gram never seem to judge me? Why was her door always open, her peace ready to be shared? What had I done to deserve that?

One evening we sat talking in the living room. My self-recrimination must have been especially evident. "Elizabeth," said Gram softly, "remember what I told you long ago—that I come from a broken home too. And believe me, if you think divorce these days is difficult, it was even worse back when my parents did it. I spent a lot of time alone as a child. That's when I learned to seek Jesus' companionship. Call on Him, Elizabeth. He'll never abandon you."

I wanted to believe that. But of course God loved Gram. She was so good!

Days turned to weeks and Gram gradually declined. Four months after I arrived, she was put on hospice care. Christmas approached. Often the house was dark and silent when I put Gram to bed. One night I wheeled her to her room and got her settled. "Let's read from *Daily Light*," she said. I opened the devotional and read the day's Scripture passage from Zephaniah: "The Lord thy God in the midst of thee is mighty; he will save, he will rejoice over thee with joy; he will rest in his love, he will joy over thee with singing."

Gram lay against her pillows contemplating these words. Finally she asked me to turn out the light so we could pray. Gram's prayers were formal and old-fashioned, full of thees and thous. "Our Heavenly Father," she began, her voice a little more tremulous than usual, "we thank Thee; we know that Thou art available, Lord, willing to hear us if we are to call upon Thee. Let us be faithful in calling, receiving Thy answers, and in letting Thee speak to us according to Thy will. We thank Thee for all things good that come from Thy hand. In Jesus' name, amen." The room was silent. I heard her wavering breath. She had fallen asleep.

For a moment I sat still, not wanting to make noise creaking across the floor. Suddenly I remembered another dark night years before, in the group home. It was one of my earliest memories. I was a toddler, cradled in Gram's lap late at night. For some reason I hadn't been able to sleep and she had come in to comfort me. I looked up at her and saw, shining in the gloom, streaks of tears down Gram's face. "Why are you crying, Gram?" I asked.

"Oh, Elizabeth," she sighed, "I am tired, dear. But I will stay up with you." And she began to sing me a lullaby.

Now I was the tired one sitting in the dark. And in a rush it came to me what had enabled Gram to love me all these years without stinting and without judgment. It wasn't some kind of spiritual heroism. It was that moment in her own childhood when she called out to Jesus and then sought His companionship ever after. Gram's love was a gift of faith. It was God loving through her. God loving me. I had thought that I was unlovable, especially by God. Here was Gram proving me wrong. And here I was proving myself wrong! I was taking care of Gram. I was returning that unstinting love. Gram was right. Love is for keeps.

Finally I got up and quietly slipped out of the room, shutting the door behind me.

The next morning I went to Gram's room to wake her. I pushed open the door and was surprised to see her sitting in her chair. Her chin rested on her chest. Her body was slightly slumped. It took me a moment to realize that she had somehow gotten up in the middle of the night to sit in her chair and had passed away.

I didn't cry. Not then, anyway. I knew God was rejoicing over her. She was resting in His love. And at last, I was too.

38.

Heading Home
by Tommy Smith

MY MIND WAS CHURNING AS I MANEUVERED MY EIGHTEEN-WHEELER THROUGH FREEWAY TRAFFIC AND HEADED EAST ON INTERSTATE 80 OUTSIDE OF YOUNGSTOWN, OHIO. I WAS SURE I WAS THE MOST MISERABLE TRUCKER ON THE ROAD THAT HOT DAY IN AUGUST 1988. JUST MINUTES EARLIER I'D LEFT A PAY PHONE AT A NOISY TRUCK STOP. MY WIFE, LADORIS, HAD TOLD ME THAT THE DIVORCE PAPERS WOULD BE READY FOR MY SIGNATURE WHEN I RETURNED HOME ON SATURDAY.

"I just can't reach you anymore, Tom," LaDoris had said, her voice trembling as she hung up.

In the side mirror I noticed a two-door, silver Oldsmobile Cutlass begin to ease around me. The driver, a slight, gray-haired woman, was leaning forward, gripping the steering wheel as she peered over the top of it at the winding road. Something about her tense posture worried me. I slowed to let her pass, and watched the Cutlass inch ahead.

My thoughts, however, kept going back to the various problems that had slowly created the trouble between LaDoris and me. It had always been hard for me to go home late on Friday night after a long stretch on the road and be ready to jump instantly into the active pace of a normal family life. For years I'd tried because I loved my family. But when I felt my wife was expecting too much of me, I began to clam up.

I even stayed away from church. LaDoris, like most of the members in our small church, wanted to be there every time the door was open, but I figured God didn't need my presence, or my off-key singing, to know that I believed in Him. When LaDoris nagged me about it, I kept my mouth shut. Finally I stopped going entirely.

Something about that Olds Cutlass caught my attention again. I watched its right turn signal begin to blink. The woman was ahead of me now and edging back into my lane. The Youngstown city limits had faded behind us, and traffic was thinning. Broiling sunlight poured into my cab and glinted off the back window of the Cutlass.

I checked the side mirror again; no one was behind me. Then I reached to flip the air-conditioner switch up a notch.

But my hand stopped in midair. My eyes were on the Cutlass again. Instead of straightening, the car veered right.

"No, lady, straighten up!" I yelled. I began applying my brakes and my tires squealed. The car struck a barricade, shot into the air, dropped down a closed freeway ramp, flipped over, and landed upright in a ditch.

"She's got a ruptured gas line!" I shouted to myself as flames appeared underneath the car. "That car's going to blow! I've got to get that woman out of there!" I skidded to a stop on the shoulder of the road, tumbled out of the truck, leaped over the guardrail, and scrambled down the embankment. *Hurry! Hurry!* I raced across the parched grass in the ditch to the car. Already it was beginning to fill with thick, black smoke.

The woman was leaning against the front side window, unconscious, still securely fastened with her seat belt. Her face was bloody. I took a deep breath and yanked open the door. As fresh air rushed in, smoke billowed out around me. I leaned in to free the woman, and an acrid smell of burning vinyl assaulted my nose. My eyes watered. Flames were beginning to lick out around the front passenger seat. I could hear a sizzling noise as I fumbled with her seat belt.

"Come on, lady, we've got to get out of here!" I could hear a crackling sound underneath the car and smelled gasoline. I knew I had only three or four minutes at the most to free her.

I tugged at the seat belt. It was jammed. Frantically I fiddled with the clasp, then pulled. Nothing happened. Coughing and panting, I fished in my pocket and pulled out my pocketknife.

"Come on. Come on!" I could only mutter the words. My mouth was so dry that my tongue was sticking to the roof of it. I hacked away at the seat belt as the heat increased on my face and hands. *Please. Please. Why doesn't somebody stop and help us?*

Finally the belt gave way in my hands. I pulled the woman out, and the car door snapped shut. I scooped her up in my arms and ran toward the truck. *At last! Now I can call for help on the CB.*

As I reached the truck, I set the woman down on the grass at the top part of the embankment. I was relieved to see that, even though part of her cheekbone was protruding through her swelling flesh, she was breathing well.

Just then her swollen eyelids began to flutter. For a moment she stared at me with a dazed expression. Suddenly her eyes widened in fear as full consciousness returned. "Did you get Philip?"

"Don't worry, ma'am, I'll call your family as soon as I get you some help."

"No, no, you don't understand. My husband! Philip was lying down in the backseat of the car!" She tried to sit up but fell back.

Oh no! In the backseat of the car! And that car can't have more than two minutes left.

"I'll get him," I croaked, hoping it was the truth.

This time, my feet felt like lead as I stumbled down the embankment and ran across the ditch to the car.

The door handle on the driver's side felt hot as I yanked the door open. The front passenger's seat was blazing. Once again, fresh air chased billows of black smoke around me.

"Philip!" I yelled, I heard a faint moan. *He's alive!* I yanked the top of the driver's seat forward and leaned over into the back. The smoke had cleared enough for me to see.

The man was upside down, behind the seat, his shoulders against the floorboard, his head under the driver's seat. The rest of his body jutted upward on the backseat, his right foot pressed against the back window, his left leg at a sickening angle halfway underneath him. His arms hung like broken tree limbs. He looked like a large, discarded rag doll.

I'm a fairly big man. He was bigger. *How am I going to get him out of here by myself? Please, somebody, help me!*

Still leaning in from outside the car, I began pulling on Philip's shoulders. I grunted and tugged, but his head was wedged so tightly it just wouldn't move. Smoke was building up again. My lungs ached. My ears buzzed.

I straightened up from my leaning position and took another gulp of fresh air. *It's no use; I can't get him out this way. I've got to get in the car. If I can just loosen up the seat enough to free his head—* It was a desperate plan, but I knew I only had seconds left.

I crawled in and straddled the bent-over driver's seat, jamming my left foot down by the floor shift. Steadying myself by holding the seat, with my right foot on the back floorboard and pressing against Philip's right shoulder, I awkwardly grabbed the bottom of the seat and pulled upward. Nothing.

I pulled again. I could feel the heat from the burning passenger seat.

It's no use. I just can't do it. And this car's going to go up in flames any time.

"God!" My scream tore from the innermost part of my being. "Please! I don't want to get out of this car without this poor man!"

Before the words cleared my lips, I knew—I knew—He was there. I could feel His divine presence filling me, giving me strength.

Once again, I pulled. I heard a *click*. The seat loosened! I pulled it forward as far as I could, then reached down and grabbed Philip under his armpits. As I pulled him up, I felt myself falling out of the car, with Philip on top of me. I stood up, picked him up in my arms, and carried him bodily along the grassy ditch and up the embankment. Exhausted, I eased him down beside his wife.

Just then the car exploded. The force of it knocked me down beside Philip. I pulled myself up to my knees and leaned over him. *He's not breathing!*

I'd never had training in resuscitation, but I knew I had to try to help him breathe. I'd seen it done in the movies. I placed my mouth on

Philip's and began to blow. Then I gently pressed his chest. Blow and press. Blow and press.

Philip began to sputter. Then stopped. "No! Philip! You can't die on me, man, not after all this! God, don't let him die!"

Blow. Press. He began to breathe again. This time, he kept breathing. And by then another trucker had arrived and was calling the police and paramedics.

Soon there were sirens and flashing lights. A paramedic checked me. Half of my beard was gone, singed from the heat. I had minor burns on my left arm, but I was fine. Hoses spewed foam on the blazing car.

As one ambulance took off for the hospital with Philip, a paramedic called me over to the side of the second ambulance. "She won't let me leave until she talks to you."

I leaned over the woman. "For as long as I live," she said, "a day won't go by that I won't say a prayer for you."

Then the ambulance was screaming away, and I turned and looked at the charred car. There on the back bumper, I saw a bright yellow sticker untouched by the fire. It proclaimed, *I Love God.*

An hour before, I had believed in God, but now I had experienced Him. I silently mouthed the words, "I love God." Then I said them out loud, "I love God." And the speaking of the words released a strong surge of joy. "I do love You, God!"

LaDoris and I didn't sign divorce papers when I got home on Saturday. We talked. And talked. We made a pledge to work things out—with the help of the same powerful God Who had become so real to me. That Sunday, I went before our congregation and asked their support for LaDoris and me.

And we've done it. Nowadays when I get home after a long trip, I'm still tired, but I don't clam up or skip church the way I used to. Whenever I'm pressed and feel like backing off, I recall my experience out there on Interstate 80, and I picture that yellow bumper sticker with three words: *I Love God.* I tell God I love Him and ask Him to help me. And just as He did out there on the interstate, He gives me strength.

One night several weeks after all of this happened, I got a phone call from the woman I'd rescued, Agnes Studer. She and Philip, a retired couple from Maryland, were slowly recovering.

LaDoris got on the phone and told her about our changed lives. And about what that bumper sticker had meant to me. When she hung up, LaDoris had a strange expression on her face.

"What is it, honey?" I asked.

"Tom, she says there was no bumper sticker on her car. And there never has been."

But it was there. I'm sure of it. For a few brief, shining moments, that bumper sticker was there. Just for me.

39.

Miracle in the Snow

by Leyla Nordby

OUTSIDE THE WINDOW, A BRANCH CREAKED MOURNFULLY. WITH THE WIND CHILL, IT WAS GOING TO HIT 37 DEGREES BELOW ZERO TONIGHT, THE TV WEATHERMAN HAD SAID. COLD EVEN BY CANADIAN STANDARDS. I PULLED THE COMFORTER UP AND SNUGGLED CLOSER TO MY TWO DAUGHTERS, HOPING THEY WERE COMFORTABLE ENOUGH TO FALL ASLEEP IN A STRANGE BED. ELSIE, MY TWO-YEAR-OLD, WAS NEXT TO THE WALL, AND THIRTEEN-MONTH-OLD ERIKA LAY IN HER DIAPER, SAFELY SANDWICHED BETWEEN US. "STILL AWAKE, BABY?" I WHISPERED, WRAPPING MY ARMS AROUND HER AND BREATHING IN HER SWEET SMELL. "DON'T WORRY, MOMMA'S HERE TO KEEP YOU WARM."

Three weeks earlier, someone had broken into our apartment. They had taken everything—my money, my furniture, even the food out of the refrigerator. I couldn't stay there after that. I felt so vulnerable alone with my girls. So unprotected. My dad put us up for a week, but housing a single mom and her kids was a lot to ask of him. I moved from one friend's house to another, trying not to be a burden. That night, my friend Robin had let us stay in her daughter's room.

I rolled over and stared out the window at the moon, bright in the February sky. I was pretty tired of not having my own house. All I wanted was a place to settle down—someplace safe, where I wouldn't worry about my girls all the time. I could relax only when I had my arms around them, like I did now. Everyone said I was overprotective, but wouldn't you be too if you'd lost a child?

Ten years before, my daughter Kayla was born with a rare heart disease. I prayed and trusted that God would work a miracle. After all, He loved her every bit as much as I did. Thirty-four days later, she passed away in my arms. Part of me died that day too, a hard, bitter death. How could I trust anybody now? I pushed away the people who reached out to me—my father, my friends, the man in my life. I even pushed away God. Especially God. If He wouldn't answer this prayer, what would it take? If God hadn't loved my daughter enough to spare her, then I would make up for it by loving my children even more. I did everything I could to take care of them, worried myself sick, but still, I never felt completely secure. If only I could free myself from this pervasive fear.

I snuggled closer to Erika, listening to her gentle, steady breathing. Eventually, I drifted off to sleep.

I woke up with a start. The moon was gone from the window. The room was pitch-black. I reached out and felt Elsie's sleeping body. Erika! I sat up, patting the bed frantically. Empty. *Calm down...calm down*, I told myself, pulling on my jeans and a shirt. *She can't have gone far.* I hurried out into the hall and peered through Robin's door. No Erika. I went from room to room, calling her name. In the kitchen, the air felt cold. I flipped on the light. The back door was open. Wide open.

I stuck my head outside. The frigid air caught in my lungs. "Erika!" I cried. I stepped into the yard and sank up to my knees. A few feet away, clearly visible in the moonlight, a small dark shape lay in the snow. My baby!

I struggled over to her, barefoot but too numb with terror to feel the cold. Erika lay facedown. Her bare legs and torso were half-buried by the swirling snow. She was completely still. A scream rose from somewhere deep within me. I dropped to my knees and snatched my baby up. Her body was stiff. So stiff. I had to get her inside. I charged back to the house and stumbled into the kitchen. I pushed everything off the table and put her down. *Clunk* went her body against the wood. She was literally a block of ice. A white layer of frost covered her pale cheeks. Her lips were blue. I pressed my ear against her chest and then held my breath, listening for even the slightest heartbeat. No trace. Nothing! Then, involuntarily, like the scream, a prayer welled up. *God . . .*

No! I thought. *I can't rely on Him.*

Robin was awake now. "I called an ambulance," she said, pushing a blanket at me. "They're on their way."

I wrapped Erika tightly, holding her to me and rocking her for what seemed like an eternity. Robin hugged us both. Soon red flashing lights appeared in the windows. EMTs rushed in carrying a stretcher. I let them take Erika from me and tried to answer the questions they shouted. Why was she out there? How long was she exposed? Robin explained that the lock on the back door was broken, that the strong wind must have blown it open. I winced as the EMTs tried to insert an IV needle into Erika's arm. No go. Her veins were frozen solid. Their desperate eyes told me all I needed to know.

At the hospital, it was a long time before I could finally talk to one of the doctors. "Your daughter's body temperature dropped more than thirty degrees," he said. "She has frostbite on her fingers and toes. We might have to amputate. Her condition is dire."

He paused, making sure I was listening. "Erika's heart stopped for at least two hours. There's no way of telling what damage that caused. We just have to wait and see." Then he was gone.

I paced and paced in the waiting area, each step taking me farther and farther into a past I didn't want to revisit. The fluorescent lights, the smell of antiseptic, the doctors and nurses in their blue scrubs—they were all like bad memories. Kayla. I'd had so many dreams about that last night in the hospital with my daughter, sitting by her bedside as she slipped away from me. *I already lived through this nightmare once*, I thought. *I can't go through it again.*

I wandered out of the waiting room and through corridors full of patients and hospital personnel, until I found myself in front of an open door. I peeked inside. A wooden cross hung on the far wall, illuminated by a soft light. The chapel. I stepped in and slid onto one of the chairs. I couldn't carry the weight of this anxiety anymore—not alone. But where could I turn? God had turned His back on me before. He'd chosen to ignore my pleas. Why trust Him again now? I looked up at the cross. *He lost a child too*, I suddenly thought. He must know how I feel. Maybe instead of blaming God, I should trust Him. I hadn't prayed since the day Kayla died. Could I ask God to help me now?

One thing was clear: I could not do this alone, and no earthly force could help me. The strangest feeling came over me, as if the ice that surrounded my heart for seven bitter years was melting away.

Lord, I can't bear another child's death. I'm just not strong enough. I need Your strength. Erika needs it. Help us.

It didn't make any sense, but as I prayed, a powerful conviction took hold of me: Everything would be okay. A few hundred yards away my daughter was lying in intensive care, but the fear that had gripped me like a fist all night long suddenly loosened. I'd done the best I could to look after my baby, but in the end, it wasn't up to me whether she lived or died. Someone else was watching out for Erika, Someone Who loved her every bit as much as I did. And Who loved me just as much. I had no choice but to trust Him.

I spent the whole next day in the hospital. Every hour or so I'd hear some new piece of good news. Each seemed like a reminder from God: Remember, everything's going to be okay.

Erika's temperature returned to normal. Her heart rate grew steady. That evening a nurse led me into pediatric ICU to see Erika for the first time since I'd given her to the medics the night before. Surrounded by life-support machines, shielded by a plastic bubble that maintained her body temperature, she lay sleeping calmly, her tiny chest gently rising and falling. The same sense of peace I'd felt in the chapel the night before rushed over me. My daughter hadn't come alone through the darkness and cold; Someone had protected her, guided her. How else to explain her survival? And He would guide me too, if I trusted Him as absolutely as I loved my children. That trust would be my freedom, that safe place I'd been looking for.

Erika stayed another week in the hospital. She had a skin graft to repair the frostbite on her hands and foot, and it healed nicely. The doctors have cautioned me that there's no way of telling what the long-term effects of hypothermia might be. Somehow, I'm not worried. They all say she is as great a medical miracle as they have ever seen. I only have to hold Erika's warm hand to remember that her life is a gift from Someone Who loves her just as much as I do. And that is the greatest miracle of all.

40.

The Loner
by Susan Peoples

THE SHADOWS IN THE CANYON WERE ALREADY DEEPENING TO PURPLE BY THE TIME MY FRIEND DAVID AND I LEFT THE BITING COLD OF THE MOUNTAIN RIVER TO CLIMB BACK UP THE RIDGE TO THE MESA ABOVE, WHERE WE'D STASHED OUR HEAVY HIKING GEAR. WEARING ONLY T-SHIRTS AND JEANS, WE HAD EARLIER DESCENDED A GENTLER SLOPE TO ONE SIDE, DRAWN BY THE SIGHT OF THAT IDYLLIC VALLEY SO FAR BELOW. NOW, LOOKING UP FROM THE DUSKY CANYON FLOOR TOWARD THE LOOMING CLIFF FACE, STILL RIMMED AT THE TOP IN GOLD FROM THE RAYS OF THE SETTING SUN, WE DECIDED TO AVOID THE EASIER PATH AND TO CLIMB STRAIGHT UP INTO THE LIGHT.

The challenge suited me. I was proud of my strong, lean body—proud of my "toughness," my independence.

As we started the climb, I glanced toward David, whom I had met just a couple of weeks before. I had to admire his lean strength as he nimbly scaled that rocky wall. I felt I could like him very much if I would choose to do so, but I'd fought against the idea—was still fighting it. Any kind of closeness to another human being seemed to me to be a dangerous thing. To invite a person to come near also meant to invite emotional pain, and that I could do without. I'd watched my parents suffer through a divorce when I'd been a child, and I hadn't liked what the stress did to them, or to me. I'd decided to keep everyone at a distance, surround myself by an invisible wall. I would shut out all emotion and become totally self-sufficient.

I'd succeeded in that goal. After growing up and leaving home, I'd held several different jobs, one of them as manager of a restaurant. That, too, had been a challenge, but I'd liked being in charge of a business. Just as I liked being in charge of my own life and destiny, climbing up this cliff.

As the way grew steeper, edging toward vertical, I constantly tested the stability of the rocks before trusting them with my weight. Several times I found a rock to be loose and I searched for a different handhold or foothold before moving higher. Soon I had ascended almost two hundred feet. I glanced again toward David, seeing that he was off to one side and a little higher than I. We had only thirty or so more feet to go before reaching the top.

And then it happened. I hooked my fingers around the edge of a shelf of rock above me that I'd thought was secure, only to have it suddenly give way. With a feeling of disbelief, as though everything had gone into slow motion, I lost my balance and dropped into space, followed by a huge chunk of ledge. I heard David scream, "My God, oh my God!"

God was Someone else I'd shut out of my life. All my growing years I had attended a strict religious school where the teachers described God as an angry, vengeful Being Who would send me to hell for my sins. I didn't like that God, and I'd decided I wanted no part of Him. I'd go it alone, assuming responsibility for my own actions, instead of cowering in fear before some cruel, mythical judge.

And so, even in my present extremity, falling toward death, I did not call on God. But David continued to cry out; not in prayer, but in an agonized, involuntary repetition of the name.

Now occurred in sequence several events so incredible that I find them hard to believe to this day. I had fallen with my face toward the cliff, but my body flipped around in midair, like a cat's, so that I was facing outward. Consequently, when my feet twice touched slight protrusions in the cliff's surface, I was tilted backward, toward the cliff face, instead of being catapulted farther into space. Then my feet landed on a small ledge, barely wide enough for one person, and the only ledge on that whole cliff between me and the ground. A few inches to either side, and I would have fallen past it. Sliding between two large cacti, I came to a halt with my legs hanging over the ledge. In one more second, I should have been crushed by the falling shelf of rock, which was several cubic feet in size. Instead, just before it would have hit me, it veered inexplicably to the right, grazing my shoulder and arm as it roared past.

I hung there in a daze, clutching at my narrow perch with my left hand while watching that boulder fall away toward the canyon floor 150 feet below. David came scrambling back down the cliff, frantically calling out to me. As he drew near, I heard him breathe, "Thank God, you're alive!" And then his voice changed as he groaned, "Susan— your leg . . ."

As yet, I felt no pain. Consequently, it was with amazement that I viewed my shattered left leg. Through the tattered remnants of my jeans, I saw three holes in the flesh of my lower leg from which broken bones protruded. My foot hung twisted around at an odd angle, like the leg of a discarded doll. I turned my head away, only to see that the inside of my right arm had been sliced completely open, elbow to wrist, exposing ripped ligaments and tendons, and a rubbery length of artery—scratched but not severed—pulsing deep inside the gaping wound.

I looked back toward David and saw that he had turned dead-white. He asked me if I thought my spine was damaged. I took mental inventory of my body, trying to determine if I had internal injuries, but I just couldn't tell. At last David said, "I don't dare try to get you off this cliff alone. I'm going to have to leave you and go for help."

I knew he was right. But the initial shock that had numbed me was beginning to wear off. I was suddenly hit by pain so devastating it froze my breath.

"Hurry—just hurry," I gasped.

He scrambled away at an angle up the ridge, heading toward the mesa and the trail that would take him out of these rugged Sangre de Cristo mountains (a Spanish name meaning "Blood of Christ") toward the jeep road, far away, where we'd left our four-wheel-drive pickup truck. I knew that the nearest hospital had to be in Española, New Mexico, about twenty miles away. I also knew it would take hours for a rescue crew to hike in with a litter. The light faded fast, taking with it the last heat from the sun. I began to shiver in my thin shirt, for September nights in the high country get very cold. In the distance, I heard the rumbling thunder of an approaching storm.

As the minutes passed, the pain grew in intensity until I felt consumed by it. The storm arrived, bringing darkness and an icy rain. The surface of the ledge became slick with water and mud, so that I had to concentrate all my strength in my left arm, trying to hold on.

My mind whirled with giddiness. It would be so easy to let go and slip into that void. To die, and end the pain.

I'd recently read a book called *Life After Life* in which people who had been declared clinically dead returned to life with stories about having met a sentient light filled with love. I didn't know if such a Being existed. But if it did, it couldn't be that hateful personage called "God."

I wanted to pray to that light, but I didn't know what to call it. Finally, I did call it God, for want of a better name. I prayed for help to arrive, and for the strength to hold on until then. I said I was frightened. I said I didn't want to be alone.

And He came.

I saw no light. I heard no voice. All I can tell you is that suddenly, beside me on that ledge, there was a Presence. A Presence filled with warmth and love. I could feel strength pouring into me from that Presence, joining with, and energizing, my own fading will.

The thoughts in my mind were in my own voice, but they said, *Hold on. You can make it. You are not alone. Help will come.*

The comfort I felt in this Presence is indescribable. Whenever I would begin to fade out, something would snap me awake once more and I would discover just enough willpower left in me to pull away from the edge.

But I wanted more. I wanted the touch of a human hand. All these years, I had kept people away. Now, suspended in air on this cold cliff, crying out in pain with almost every breath, I longed desperately for someone to hold me, to talk to me, to distract me from the prison of agony my body had become.

Time flowed into a meaningless blur. And then, between my cries, I heard someone, faint and far away, calling my name. Peering down into the darkness, I saw a tiny light bobbing along the canyon floor.

I called to that light, and the light answered. I saw it veer toward me and proceed, slowly but surely, up the cliff. A face came into view over the side of the ledge, eerily white in the flashlight's glow.

It was a child. A boy about twelve or thirteen years old. I thought for a moment that I was hallucinating. But the boy scrambled up beside me on the slippery ledge. He carefully set the flashlight down in a depression in the rocks. And then he took a folded blanket from his shoulder and draped it over me, shielding me from the rain.

"Who are you?" I whispered.

"I'm Michael," he replied.

He was real. The touch of his small, dirt-roughened hands told me that. He explained that David, frantically looking for a phone, had shown up at the door of Michael's house, outside the canyon. But Mr. Browne, Michael's father, had no phone and was too ill to help with any kind of rescue effort. After hastily telling the Brownes about the accident, David had rushed away, heading once more down the mountain in his search for help.

"I thought you might be cold," Michael said, "so I came to find you."

He said he'd ridden his dirt bike until the brush got too thick. Then he'd hiked on into the canyon, and at last he'd heard my cries.

He asked what he could do for me, and I suggested that he elevate my injured arm. Surprisingly, my wounds had clotted soon after the accident, so I was no longer bleeding profusely; but elevating the arm seemed to help ease the pain. However, as we shifted on the ledge, I once more slipped toward the edge. Michael quickly grabbed my shoulders and held on, stopping my fall. After he had maneuvered me back to relative safety, he continued to hang on to me, while assuring me that the rescuers would arrive soon. He made me talk in order to keep me awake. Each time I started to slide forward on the slick surface of the ledge, Michael tightened his hold, dragging me back again. He was so determined to save me that I am convinced, had I actually gone over the edge, he would not have released his hold, but would have fallen with me to his own death.

As my mind wandered, I got to thinking that Michael might be a guardian angel. But he chattered on, like any normal boy, telling me about his friends in the Española Junior High and asking me questions just to make sure I was still with him.

I had totally lost track of time. I know now that Michael held me on that ledge for over two hours before more lights appeared in the canyon—David, with a doctor and two paramedics.

The ordeal they went through for the next several hours getting me off the cliff is another story. All I can say is that there were many acts of heroism from them all as they climbed the slippery rocks, splinting my leg and arm, strapping me into a litter, lowering me on ropes to the canyon floor. Michael acted as messenger, relaying instructions from one rescuer to another. All this in cold, wet darkness.

As groggy as I was, I still realized their terrible danger, and my prayer changed: *Please, God, don't let one of them die on this cliff, helping me.*

Because of a head injury I hadn't even known about, the doctor was not able to give me painkillers. My screams, every time I was accidentally jostled, had to be unnerving for the men, but they didn't give up. Even though they were cold and exhausted, they carried me as carefully as they could over the rough canyon floor and up the slopes to the pickup truck, then drove me over rocky jeep trails to the road where the ambulance waited. Because of the seriousness of my injuries, the doctors in Española couldn't treat me, but sent me on to St. Vincent's Hospital in Santa Fe. At last, twelve hours after my fall, I went into surgery, where the doctors pieced my torn and broken body back together.

I awoke to find myself immobilized in heavy casts. Me, Ms. Independence, totally helpless and having to rely on others for everything—bedpans, baths, food, therapy. Dozens of flower arrangements and over a hundred cards arrived, soon filling my room. Friends and acquaintances flocked to see me, saying eagerly, "You've always been such a loner, Susan, holding us off. But at last we're going to get to do something for you!"

The God I met on that ledge was neither angry nor condemning. The God I met there was love. Love, flowing from an unseen Presence to give me strength; love, coming from David and the rescue team as they struggled to get me off the cliff; love from doctors, nurses, and old friends; and love from Michael, a child who sustained me during that lonely, painful night.

When that rock fell, so did the wall I'd built around myself to shut out that love. I will never be the same.

41.

The Remaking of an Outcast

by Daniel Poling

EIGHT YEARS TO THE DAY AFTER HE WAS RELEASED FROM PRIS-ON, I HAD LUNCH WITH ROBERT BROWN. GEORGE BOLTON WAS THERE; SO WAS FRANK CARLSON. ALL OF US WERE ACTORS IN A MODERN DRAMA ILLUSTRATING ONE OF THE OLDEST PRINCIPLES OF OUR RELIGION: THERE'S ALWAYS HOPE, BECAUSE THERE IS GRACE.

What is grace? Let me tell you how Robert Brown found the answer to that question.

Robert was a walking battlefield. I'd known him all his life. He was the son of a lifelong friend of mine, and I watched his career through his parents. I knew that he was a brilliant boy who would not study; that he quit college; worked as a lumberjack out West; came East, married, had three sons, and shot to an early success as a salesman in New York. He began drinking heavily in his business. He joined Alcoholics Anonymous. For a year and a half, the battle seemed to go in his favor.

Then, suddenly, he had a severe defeat.

One day Robert decided to try that famous "just one drink to see how I can handle it now." Within a month he was consuming two quarts of liquor a day. Within six months he was fired. Within a year he deserted his wife. He gambled away a $36,000 inheritance. He began to "borrow" from his friends until he ran out of friends. Then he began to borrow from his father's friends and to pass bad checks.

One day I had an urgent call requesting an interview.

Robert walked in with an air of assurance and greeted me with an unexpectedly firm handshake. He sat down, at ease, the picture of a good salesman. He had lost his job because of a change in management. He had just heard of an excellent position in China. Would I by any chance be in a position to advance him some money to get there?

"What's happened to you, Robert?" I asked.

"What do you mean?"

"You bring me a fantastic yarn and you expect me to swallow it because I'm a minister with my head up in the clouds. Well, I'll help you if you want it. But I won't give you a penny."

"Look, Dr. Poling, if you can't help—just forget it."

I was silent. Then I reached into my pocket. Robert's eyes lit up for a moment.

But instead of money I took out a pen and wrote an address on a piece of paper. "If you want help, go to this address."

Robert looked at the paper, puzzled. On it was the address of the Bowery Mission.

"You go there," I said "and see a man named George Bolton. He's traveled the same road you're on."

Robert seemed disgusted, but folded the paper, bid me a hasty good-bye, and left. That was the last I expected to hear of Robert Brown, but I telephoned George Bolton and told him the story, just in case.

I learned later that Robert left the office angry and thirsty. The first thing he did was buy a bottle of wine. It cost him his last dollar. He took the wine into a telephone booth and drained it without stopping. Then he went to Penn Station and lay down on a bench and tried to figure out whether or not he should go down to the Bowery. He could imagine what it was like. There'd be a lot of bums trading a prayer for a bowl of soup. *But if I play along*, Robert thought, *maybe I can still get a hundred.*

So the next morning, Robert did go down to the Bowery. He saw the bums asleep on the sidewalk, and for a brief moment he saw in them his own image, like a man suddenly catching sight of himself in a street-mirror. He became embarrassed and turned away. He walked to the address on the slip of paper. There he met George Bolton who, through long experience, knew that Robert's first need was the sobering influence of food and sleep.

So Robert was fed and was given a bed in the dormitory. Then in the morning he went to George Bolton's office. Instinctively Robert knew George had, indeed, traveled the same road. There was little use putting up a front, so instead, somewhat to his surprise, Robert leveled with George Bolton. He tried for the first time, and unsuccessfully, to explain to George how he had gotten into such shape.

"It was just in the cards, I guess," Robert said. He told of all the struggles to control himself. The more he struggled, the further he seemed to slip downhill.

George Bolton listened. After a while, he tried something:

"Have you ever heard of grace?" he asked.

"Grace? It sounds like one of those hollow religious words."

"Grace is unmerited mercy."

"Why are you telling me this?"

"You've tried the rest, now try the best. Relax and ask for help from the grace of God."

God can enter a man's heart in a split second, in the mere twinkling of an eye. Although he didn't understand how it was to affect him, Christ came into Robert's life then and there—at George Bolton's desk in the Bowery.

Robert rose to his feet and shook George Bolton's hand and then walked out to the street and uptown to Penn Station. His first action, as a new man, must be to square accounts, to face the warrant for his arrest on a charge of non-support.

He borrowed a coin from a newsie and phoned the police.

For days, while he was awaiting trial, he sat benumbed in his cell. He refused to see anyone. Robert was ordered by the judge to pay his wife a weekly amount. Immediately on his release, he was arrested again for the bad checks he had passed months before. He was sentenced to six months in the county jail in Mineola, New York.

The life at Mineola was hard. Robert was assigned to the kitchen. He worked from 4:30 in the morning to 7:30 at night. He worked silently, the fog of confusion and alcohol still clouding his brain. But a phrase kept beating through his mind: "You've tried the rest; now try the best."

One day, while he plodded through his chores with the phrase tumbling around inside his head, he drew himself a cup of prison coffee. It was foul. He looked at the coffee urn. It was coated with a brown crust from a thousand improper washings.

This urn is just like me, he thought. *How can I turn out good coffee with tools like this? How can I straighten myself out with my own tools corroded? You've tried the rest; now try the best. Maybe I'll give this urn some unmerited mercy. I'll clean it.*

During his six months in jail Robert spent literally hundreds of hours scouring the urn with steel wool and baking soda. He identified himself completely with his job, and as he worked, he began quietly to pray as he had learned to do as a child. He asked that, by the grace of God, he might be cleaned too.

The day for his release arrived. The prison warden, who had watched Robert working for such long hours on the urn, said goodbye. "I'm going to miss the good coffee," the warden said. "When I say I hope never to see you again, you know what I mean."

Robert tried to get a job in New York. No one would take a chance on him. He was tempted briefly to visit a Long Island gambler he had met in prison, who once offered him an underworld job. Instead, Robert telephoned the Bowery Mission.

"I want to see you," said George Bolton. "Right away."

When Robert arrived, Bolton introduced an old friend, Frank Carlson. Mr. Carlson and Robert talked for a long time and before the interview was over, Robert Brown, the crack salesman, had accepted a day-labor job at Carlson's warehouse.

Immediately, Robert began sending three-fourths of his pay home to his wife. She inquired after him, passed word along that she wanted to see him. Both agreed not to see each other too often at first.

"I want to make it my own way," said Robert.

"What about—your drinking?"

"It's been seven months now."

"Good luck, Robert. I'll be praying."

"And so," said Robert, "will I."

Robert worked as a day-laborer for well over a year. He was relaxed. An old school chum, a man high in the echelons of one of America's great corporations, learned about Robert's change and offered him work.

"No thanks," said Robert. "I have to go slowly. I'll call you."

After a year and three months of steady, hard day-labor, Robert did call. "I believe I've worked my way through," said Robert. What he meant was simple. He had, during his test year, organized his own, slow program of rehabilitation. For one thing he was going to pay back every dollar he had stolen. Then there was the question of alcohol. He had conquered it. There was also his program of prayer, which by now was a deeply entrenched habit. And there was his wife.

On the next Thanksgiving day Robert ordered a turkey, carried it out to his wife and children. It was an old-fashioned, home Thanksgiving, and then Robert heard the words he'd been waiting for.

"What do you think?" his wife asked. "Should we try it again?"

That's about the end of the story. Robert went back with his wife. As we were all having lunch on the eighth anniversary of his release from jail, Robert told me those years had been, for the most part, truly rewarding. He and his wife were happy. He had an excellent job as sales manager of one of America's largest companies and had tried to make restitution to everyone he had harmed. He was at ease. He felt sure he would never take one—not one—step backward.

What is grace? Grace is the free favor of God toward men. It is our hope when all else has failed.

42.

Bottle of Tears
by Carol Virgil

DARTING AROUND THE HOUSE, RACING TO BEAT THE GARBAGE MAN TO THE CURB, I EMPTIED MY DAUGHTER ELIZABETH'S WASTE-BASKET. A CRUMPLED PIECE OF PAPER FELL TO THE FLOOR. SOMETHING ABOUT IT CAUGHT MY EYE, AND I SMOOTHED OUT THE PAGE. THE WORLD SEEMED TO SHIFT INTO SLOW MOTION AS ELIZABETH'S HANDWRITING CAME INTO FOCUS.

I hate myself. I hate myself. I hate myself.

The ugly words had been scrawled again and again, filling half the page. I heard the garbage truck next door. I heard the bang of garbage cans. But I couldn't make myself move.

Elizabeth, the middle of my three daughters, had always been a bit melodramatic. Recently she had confided, "Mom, I think I'm losing my mind." I had not been overly concerned. Most teenagers go through phases of insecurity. But while staring at the paper, I realized something was frighteningly wrong.

When she got home that day, I asked if anything particular had been bothering her. I didn't mention the paper I had found. She admitted feeling unhappy, and I suggested she talk to the counselor at our church. She did, and by the time summer rolled around she seemed back to normal. I figured Elizabeth's sensitive nature was magnifying the usual storms of adolescence.

Several months later, in the middle of her junior year, she walked in the door one day exclaiming, "Oh, my head hurts!" She tossed her schoolbooks on the couch, then began to groan and bang her head against the wall.

I ran to her and threw my arms around her. "Elizabeth! That isn't going to do your headache any good."

"Maybe not," she said, "but it feels good to have a different kind of pain for a change."

My husband, Lyle, and I took her to the doctor, but he couldn't find any physical cause for her recurring headaches. I hoped with summer vacation coming whatever was bothering her would go away.

Elizabeth spent the summer in California working on a film. When she called home to tell us about her adventures, she sounded like she was having fun. Maybe her problems were behind her.

In July a friend and I drove to pick Elizabeth up. She was flying high, so high I was alarmed. She loved California! She loved working on the movie! "Mom, I got to be an extra! I even got a speaking part in a classroom scene!"

"Elizabeth seems a lot happier than she did a couple months ago," my friend said later.

"I know," I answered, "but I've seen her bouncing-off-the-wall happy before. She has nowhere to go emotionally but down."

Elizabeth maintained her high through the beginning of the school year. Then in mid-October she crashed. It was her senior year. She should have been having the time of her life. But she lost all interest in her activities. She started crawling into bed right after getting home from school and sleeping for hours on end. She was miserable. Lyle and I were miserable for her.

We didn't understand what was wrong. All we knew to do was to pray. Yet turning to God didn't seem to bring Elizabeth—or us—any relief.

One day, just before the holidays, Elizabeth slid a note across the kitchen counter toward me.

Elizabeth's Christmas List
MY SANITY

"Oh, Elizabeth, is it that bad?" I asked. I was afraid to hear her answer.

"Sometimes I even have trouble breathing," she whispered, tears gathering in her eyes. "I feel like I'm being buried alive."

I squeezed her hand.

"I know I'm not normal," she said. "Mom, please, you've got to get me some help."

For the first time I understood Elizabeth's emotional anguish was as real as any physical pain—and maybe more devastating.

Right after Christmas we took her to see a psychiatrist. He made the diagnosis: clinical depression. "Your daughter needs medication," he said, "the sooner, the better." This wasn't an adolescent phase. We were dealing with a serious mental illness.

We hoped the medication would ease her depression. Instead, she became agitated, suspicious, even irrational at times. One February afternoon I was working at my computer when Elizabeth walked by, dressed in her Wendy's uniform.

"I'm leaving for work," she said.

"Is it that late already?" I asked. "What time are you off?" It was a run-of-the-mill conversation. Nothing in my daughter's words or manner gave any hint that she had just swallowed an entire bottle of antidepressants.

Lyle and I were at a party when we got the call. Elizabeth had been rushed to the emergency room. We have wonderful friends; everyone at the party showed up at the hospital to support and pray for us.

"One pill a day didn't seem to do any good," Elizabeth explained dully, looking disconsolate in her hospital bed. "I thought more would make it work faster." Fortunately, she hadn't taken enough to do permanent damage.

I cried all that night, and many others after we brought her home. I didn't know where to turn. Intellectually I knew God was there for us, but I just couldn't feel it. Not in my heart.

Elizabeth soon plummeted into such despair that nothing could pull her out. She disappeared without letting anyone know where she was going. She told her boyfriend she didn't have anything to live for.

Her psychiatrist put her on a different medication. Her condition only deteriorated. By then Elizabeth had lost twenty pounds. Sometimes just looking at her made me cry. Her expression said it all: her life was misery.

"I think we need a second opinion," I told Lyle, desperate. "Remember that advice program we used to listen to on Christian radio? A clinic ran it. I'd feel better putting Elizabeth in the care of people who use faith in their counseling."

We found a clinic-affiliated doctor nearby and took Elizabeth to see him. "Medication is important," he said, "but alone it isn't usually enough." He recommended that she be placed in their hospital program in Seattle for intensive therapy. We made plans for her to enter the clinic Monday morning right after her graduation, only a week away. All of us, including Elizabeth, knew she wouldn't be able to hang on much longer than that.

But first we had to get through her graduation weekend. "Lord," I prayed, "don't You know how much my family is suffering? Please help us make it to Monday somehow."

Our doorbell rang Saturday morning before commencement. It was Jeanne, a woman from our church we didn't know well. "I'm not sure why I'm here," she said, looking sheepish. "But I had a strong feeling God wanted me to bring you this."

She handed Lyle a clear glass bottle with a cork in the top. Hanging from a ribbon threaded through a metal ring in the cork was a tag with an excerpt from Psalm 56:8.

"'You have collected all my tears and preserved them in Your bottle,'" Lyle read. "Jeanne, did you know what was going on with our family?" he asked, giving me the bottle.

Jeanne shook her head. "This verse has always meant a lot to me," she said. "If I'm having a tough time, it reminds me that God sees every single one of my tears. When I get to heaven, I expect Him to hand me the bottle and say, 'Welcome, and cry no more.'"

Clutching that bottle, I felt God truly with us. For the first time in months I sensed His love, warm and deep. Jeanne reminded me that God had been paying attention all along, but I had been too caught up in our family's emotional upheavals to recognize it. He cared so much, loved us so much, that He hadn't missed a single one of our tears—Elizabeth's or mine. God loves us no less than we love our own children. How could I ever have lost sight of that?

Elizabeth was admitted as scheduled to the clinic. She came home calmer, on different medication, and with some newfound coping skills, including using her faith to help work through her despair. Eventually she was diagnosed with bipolar disorder. There is no overnight cure. Elizabeth has a long way to go before she learns to live with her illness. So do I. But we have found peace and hope in the assurance that God is there for us, collecting our tears as they fall. In our darkest times, I cling to that thought, for now I know it in my heart.

43

When God Touched My Life

by Rhonda Fleming

WHEN I WAS EIGHTEEN YEARS OLD, I HAD AN EXPERIENCE THAT WAS TO AFFECT THE REST OF MY LIFE.

My parents were divorced. Starved for family love, I ran away at sixteen to marry my childhood sweetheart. At seventeen, I had my precious son. Then the war came along, and soon my young husband was drafted and sent overseas. During his long absence, I lived with his very religious parents in Hollywood, the town where I was born.

One day an agent who had "discovered" me on my way to Beverly Hills High School called and invited me to meet producer David O. Selznick, who immediately signed me to a seven-year contract and placed me in a top featured role with Ingrid Bergman and Gregory Peck in *Spellbound*.

This was a real Hollywood-Cinderella story. I had had no training as an actress; I had never had to pound the New York or Hollywood pavements looking for a job; it was simply handed to me without my even asking for it. It should have been a happy and exciting time for me, but instead I was troubled by deep insecurities. Here I was—

estranged from my own family, my soldier-husband gone for over a year—a young, inexperienced, naive girl suddenly being groomed and flattered and written about and sometimes chased by older, sophisticated men. I was both frightened and terribly lonely. I had no friend to talk to, no counselor to advise me. When the studio would arrange "dates" for me with other young actors to attend premieres for publicity, I was told never to reveal that I was married and certainly never to mention that I had a baby. Even my real name was changed!

All of these things were upsetting. To make matters worse, I became more and more estranged from my in-laws. Though they were helping me with my son, I was living a life they did not understand or really approve of. More and more, I sank into depression. Some of my thoughts were close to suicidal. One of the other young girls under contract had recently taken her own life, and I was despondent over that.

One night, after driving around for hours by myself, not wanting to go home because I felt nothing for these people with whom I was living (in fact, I felt no love for anything or anyone, including myself, except for my little baby), I was close to despair as I finally parked my jalopy on a hill overlooking the lights of Hollywood. It was a warm night, and yet I was so cold my teeth were chattering; I felt as though I had ice water flowing through my veins. I didn't want to go on living.

All through my childhood, my mother had dragged me to church, and thank the Lord she did, because now, out of sheer desperation, I cried out from the depths of my soul: "I've always been told there's a God—so if You are real, God, then hear me now because I don't want to live."

I don't know how long I sat there staring out over the dark outlines of barren hills, tears streaming down my face, begging God to hear me, when suddenly I felt what seemed to be the firm pressure of a hand placed upon my head. From that pressure, heat came surging through my body, melting the ice in my veins, and with it came a tremendous love that was so full and powerful that I couldn't wait to start my car and share that love with someone. I found myself racing home to that little house and awakening my in-laws just to tell them I loved them. "I love you, I love you," I repeated over and over, and startled as they were, they were quick to say, "We love you too." Then

I hugged my little son with this newfound love and slept peacefully for the first time in months.

How privileged I was to experience the presence of the Holy Spirit, to have been "touched" by God in direct answer to my prayerful plea! I shall never forget it. Nothing can ever take that experience from me; it has changed my life, knowing that He does hear us and all we need to do is ask and we will receive His blessings.

We are not alone: "Behold, I stand at the door, and knock: if any man hear My voice and open the door, I will come in" (Revelation 3:20).

He has come into my heart to stay forever, and I hope that telling this story will help others to seek His help. Never forget: He is our best friend—and "with God all things are possible" (Matthew 19:26).

Night of Fear

by Malcolm Jones

WE WERE FLYING OVER THE MOONLIT FLORIDA EVERGLADES THAT JANUARY EVENING, ON OUR WAY HOME TO KEY WEST AFTER A BUSINESS CONFERENCE IN FT. LAUDERDALE. "I USED TO HUNT DOWN THERE IN THE EVERGLADES WHEN I WAS A BOY," I SAID TO BILL LINDSEY, WHO WAS PILOTING OUR SMALL PLANE.

Bill looked below at the swampland. He gave a shudder. "No thanks," he said. "I'm not that fond of alligators or crocodiles."

Up ahead a white cloud appeared in the sky. It was strange looking; it almost seemed to glow. I started to tell Bill something about alligators, but he was peering intently at that cloud. We flew into it and immediately the buffeting began. "I don't like this," Bill said.

Suddenly the plane dropped out from under us. Bill pulled back on the controls, but the plane did not respond. "We're in a twister!" Bill yelled. Suddenly the grassy swamp appeared out of the cloud, rushing up at us with great speed.

When I came to, I realized that I was lying facedown on the ripped-out door of the plane. It was half-floating in a shallow, grass-choked lake. I saw in the moonlight that the bone of my left thumb was sticking out through the skin. My left foot and rib cage were numb. There were probably broken bones too.

Then I remembered Bill. I lifted my head and looked around. Twenty-five feet away were the remains of our plane, its engine ripped out, its wing torn off.

And there, near the plane, was Bill's body. All I could see was his head and shoulders, sticking out of the shallow lake. It took all my energy to hobble over to Bill and pull his head up out of the water. He groaned, and then gasped. He was alive!

Taking Bill by the shoulders, I dragged him backward, inch by panting inch, until we reached the plane. It took me twenty minutes to hoist him up onto that wing. I knew that Bill was in severe shock.

"Got to keep him warm," I said to the night. Inside the plane I found clothing with which I wrapped Bill, but he continued to shake. "Lord," I said, "we've got to find help or Bill will die."

Then I realized that I was praying! It immediately made me feel like a hypocrite. There had been a time when prayer and the Bible were the dynamics of my life, but that time had passed. How could I suddenly begin praying again now when I was in trouble? While thinking these thoughts, I remembered the Bible verse: "Lo, I am with you always" (Matthew 28:20).

It came with such extraordinary clarity that I actually looked around to see if anyone was there.

Suddenly my thoughts were interrupted. Because far out in the swamp, just visible at the waterline, were two green candles. I knew instantly what they were: alligator eyes.

"Never go near an alligator nest," the old-timers used to tell me. "The mother will attack."

I had been hoping we were in a part of the swamp too shallow for the alligators. Now I found myself thinking of all sorts of reasons why I should not go looking for help. Search planes would be out at daybreak. Bill might need me here. I was in shock myself. I had broken bones. But to each argument came one simple answer: by leaving the plane I'd double our chances of being found.

As soon as it was daylight, I dug out our maps. Off to the southwest was a straight line: that would be a drainage canal and highway. If I could just get there.

I wanted to get a fire going so smoke would rise over the wreckage, but nowhere could I find a match. It was late morning when I gave Bill all the water he would drink, explained as carefully as possible to him where I was going, and got what I thought was a nod of understanding.

There wasn't an alligator or a crocodile in sight as I started out. But the shallow part of the swamp lasted only a short while. Very soon I came to deeper pits and swamp lakes, which I knew could be gator breeding grounds. Then, they would give out and I'd be sloshing my way through a marsh with saw grass nine feet tall, its needles ripping through my light sports coat.

Within an hour I was panting and sweating. By mid-afternoon, I was exhausted, and by dusk I was aching with fatigue. I tried to find a tree or some brush strong enough to carry my weight: every time I climbed into one I sank right down into the black water. Laboriously, as the last light faded, I built a little mound of swamp grass and twigs and tried to lie down on it but it slowly sank.

Now it was totally dark. The moon was not out yet. It began to drizzle. The temperature fell into the low forties. I was shivering and I knew I had no choice but to keep moving.

Once again, amid the night smells and noises of the swamp, I headed southwest. Each step now was an aching torture.

"I can't go on," I said, fighting off sleep. But I did go on.

Then, suddenly, not twenty feet away, I saw the thing I'd been dreading most: green eyes in the dark!

They were directly in front of me—about ten inches apart—and they did not move. And then, I saw, just off to the right, another set of eyes, much smaller. It was a mother and her young, the most dangerous combination in the swamp.

The alligator bellowed loudly. And suddenly there was a terrifying chorus of bellowing. I swung around. There were more eyes to my right, my left, behind me!

I froze. Twenty minutes passed, and then, slowly, with only the slightest sound, the ring of alligators began to press in on me.

"What am I going to do, Lord?"

Fear not. I am with you.

And once again, I knew precisely what it was I had to do: walk slowly and purposefully, right through that circle of eyes.

I started to move. The eyes moved too. I inched forward and they followed, bellowing to each other all the while. The water grew deeper, as it does where the alligators dig out nests with their tails.

"Steady now," I said, and a bellowing answered back. "Steady. I'm going to come through and you will get out of the way. I'm leaving your home and you're not going to bother me."

I walked right toward those eyes.

And at the last possible moment, they broke. The beast turned and with a lazy sound slithered off.

All that night, praying, I lived with the alligators of the Everglades swamps. I must have walked through a dozen nests. I saw many young alligators. But I was never bothered by any of them.

Shortly after dawn, the first planes came by. I waved and shouted but they did not see me. An hour later, more planes swept over, and again I jumped and waved and called: no one saw me. It wasn't until I finally asked the Lord what I should do that it dawned on me to take off my sports jacket. That coat was acting as a perfect camouflage.

When the next plane came by, I had my jacket off and was waving my white shirt as a flag.

This time the plane circled. Half an hour later, a helicopter picked me up and we headed toward the hospital. Bill, I learned to my relief, had been found alive just half an hour earlier. But below I saw the canal I'd been searching for and I knew that if the plane had not spotted Bill I'd have been able to get help to him before the day was out.

There was a long delay while doctors set bones, asked questions, probed, fussed, and talked about how remarkable it was that I was alive. But finally I was allowed to see my wife, Hellen. After I had told her my story, I asked her to go find a Bible.

During the time I was in the swamp, I had a persistent feeling there was something I was supposed to learn from this experience. I kept thinking about the story in Hebrews about people exactly like me. People who had once been close to God but who had stopped growing. I asked Hellen to read from the Book of Hebrews. While she was reading the fifth chapter, I stopped her and had her reread this verse: "Though by this time you ought to be teachers, you need someone to teach you the elementary truths of God's word all over again. You need milk, not solid food!" (Hebrews 12:5).

This was my answer.

It was in a time of disaster that God led me through kindergarten once again and fed me on spiritual milk. For it was there that I relearned the heartwarming, basic fact of Christian life: that although at times we may turn cold toward God, He is with us always, just waiting for an opportunity to come back into our lives.

45.

The Taming of Tariri

by James Hefley

IT WAS AN UNBELIEVABLE SITUATION. TWO YOUNG AMERICAN GIRLS, LED BY A NATIVE GUIDE NAMED GUITERREZ, HAD TRAVELED FOR SIX HOURS BY CANOE THROUGH PERU'S REMOTE JUNGLE. NOW THEY HAD REACHED THEIR DESTINATION: THE UNTAMED SHAPRA TRIBE, WHOSE CHIEF, TARIRI NOCHOWATA, WAS THE MOST FEARED HEAD-HUNTER IN A VAST FIVE-RIVER AREA. AS THE CANOE TOUCHED THE BANK, A ROW OF SAVAGES STARED AT THE GIRLS WITH DARK FROWNS.

The two slender white girls—Doris Cox and Lorrie Anderson—climbed out to face a big savage who stood before them in regal splendor. Two thick shocks of black hair drooped to his waist. Links of colored beetle earrings hung below his shoulders. Strings of colored beads rattled across his broad chest.

"Him, Tariri, big chief of five rivers," the native guide whispered to the girls. Doris and Lorrie tensed. Before them stood the bandit chief who had defied the Peruvian army, a man who beheaded his enemies, then shrunk their heads as trophies of his prowess.

"Great Brother, we have come to live with your people and to learn your language." The white girls spoke in sign language and the few Shapra words they had learned from the down-river trader.

Dirty, naked children pranced excitedly behind Tariri and his warriors. For a long tense silence, no one spoke. Then Tariri moved, rattling the beads on his chest, and waved the girls into the village. "Welcome, sisters," he said, although at the time the girls did not understand what he meant.

Providentially, they had called Tariri "brother"—the one Shapra word that obligated him and his tribe to protect them. Tariri later said, "Had men come we would have speared them on sight. Had a married couple come I would have killed the man and taken the woman for my hut. But two helpless girls came, calling me brother. I was bound to defend them. I felt they were harmless and probably only looking for husbands."

Actually the girls were on an assignment for the Wycliffe Bible Translators to reduce the Shapra Candoshi dialect to writing for the first time, and then translate it into Scripture portions for the tribe to read. Doris Cox, a Chico, California, girl, and Lorrie Anderson, a resident of Providence, Rhode Island, made an ideal team since both had writing talent, a creative approach to the arts, and a conviction that God had called them for missionary service.

Tariri welcomed Doris Cox and Lorrie Anderson to his tribe by giving them a palm shelter and two older women to help them get settled. Many crises followed. One time Tariri's wife became ill and was unable to cook the chief's food. Tariri informed the girls that he was going wife-hunting; a simple matter of killing a husband and bringing the wife back to the village.

"Oh no," the girls protested. "The God Who made the jungle, sun, and sky doesn't want this. We'll cook your food until your wife is better."

Tariri grunted in assent, put down his spear and blowgun, and motioned to the cooking pot.

Doris and Lorrie knew what they must do. Tariri's food was made by chewing boiled yucca roots and mixing with saliva to become a soupy mixture. But unlike the Indian women who used a communal kettle, the fastidious girls deposited their product in separate kettles.

"Our jaws got terribly sore," they said later when they could laugh. "You can't imagine how hard we prayed for the chief's wife to get well."

Tariri's wife recovered and the girls began the tedious work of putting down the Shapra dialect, using methods they had learned at the Wycliffe training center at the University of Oklahoma. They patiently listened to Shapra gibberish, watching how the lips parted to make each speech sound. They symbolized each sound with a letter from the phonetic alphabet. The phonetic translation was then worked into a practical alphabet.

Chief Tariri, intent upon his tribal wars and hunting expeditions, left the girls to their strange activities. But he kept close tab on his new sisters through informers.

After five months, using a two-way radio as their only contact with the outside world, Doris and Lorrie noticed that Tariri and his people had become friendly—and curious. "Why do you look at that Book so often?" Tariri asked. "Why do you bow your head, close your eyes, and talk to yourself?" The girls explained that "the Book is the message of the God Who made the jungle, sun, moon, and sky. When we close our eyes we talk to Him about our brothers, the Shapras."

Three rainy seasons came and went. Doris and Lorrie toiled on in their translation work. The tribe remained committed to savagery and superstition. Wild festivals often were held in the village, sending ripples of fear racing up and down the spines of the girls. The people would drink a weird concoction made from tobacco juice that plunged them into drunken frenzies. When illness struck—as it frequently did—the Shapras would capture a boa constrictor and beg the snake to release the sick victim from its power.

Again and again Doris and Lorrie spoke to the chief about a new life. "The great God loves you, Great Brother. He wants to come into your life."

One day, after hearing this, Tariri impulsively grabbed up his blowgun and stalked off into the jungle to hunt. He said later that as he walked through the thick flora, the battle between the old and the new raged within. He was strangely drawn to the girls' God. Yet tribal customs were a part of his life.

Hours later Tariri returned to the village and stood uncertainly before the girls. Doris asked him shyly, "Will you join us as we talk to

God?" Tariri meekly knelt beside her, his beads and earrings jingling in the still jungle air.

Recalling this pivotal point in his life, Tariri now says, "When I prayed to my sisters' God, my heart became joyous. God frightened the devil in me to death. God shot me through with His sun rays."

In the months that followed, over one hundred Shapras followed their chief in accepting Christianity. In Tariri's life, the change was nothing short of amazing.

He sent jungle runners to the Agurun, Miratos, Huambisas, and Jivaro peoples—his most hated enemies. "My brothers," he said, "I have a murder record on every river. But God has forgiven me. I am a new man. My heart is full of love. Come, see if I am not telling the truth." Hesitantly, slowly, suspiciously, but surely, Tariri's old enemies came to hear the new Tariri speak. They went away puzzled.

News of Tariri's conversion reached America. He was flown to New York. There, he saw more people than he ever had imagined existed.

Before returning to the jungle, Tariri asked to meet "the head man from my country." He was taken to the Peruvian Embassy in Washington.

There in the presence of the ambassador and his staff, Tariri solemnly removed his earrings. "Mr. Ambassador," he said meekly, "I give these to you. Please tell people that they came from a chief who once took off heads in the jungle but has stopped because he loves God."

46.

Only Minutes to Live
by David Vaughn

THE STEADY BUZZING OF THE CHAIN SAW FILLED THE WOOD-
ED HOLLOW WHERE I WAS WORKING ONE COLD AFTERNOON IN
LATE OCTOBER. CUTTING MY OWN WOOD SAVED US FIVE HUN-
DRED DOLLARS IN FUEL BILLS EACH WINTER. ALTHOUGH MY
WIFE, PAM, DIDN'T LIKE MY BEING OUT IN THE WOODS ALONE, I
LOVED IT. THERE WERE NO BOSSES TO TELL ME WHAT TO DO; THE
WOODS WERE MY WORLD.

Working at a steady pace, I was warm, even in my T-shirt. The work
went fast because, long before this, I had removed the saw's safety
roller tip, which gave me an extra two inches of blade to cut through
thicker trees. In a little over an hour I had enough wood to fill the truck.

As I turned to load the truck, I noticed the cherry tree I had felled
the previous evening. It had appeared to be rotten, so I'd left it. Now
I thought, *Maybe I'll give it a cut.*

Leaning over, I pressed the whirling blade against the fallen trunk.
It sliced like butter. Then, halfway through, the chain started throwing
sparks—it had hit a piece of embedded barbed wire. The kick, when it
came, was so strong that it threw the chain saw up and back. Ducking,
I felt the razor-sharp blade whirl past, just flicking my T-shirt.

Still holding the whirring saw I thought, *Boy, that was close!* Then I felt something warm on my chest. I looked down. Blood . . .

Throwing down the saw I thought, *Good Lord! What have I done?* I knew I had to stay calm and assess the damage. As I went to look in the truck mirror, I reached up and touched my throat. It was cut! All I could think was, *I'm going to die!*

I twisted my T-shirt around my neck like a tourniquet, but it didn't help. I sat down on the tailgate of the truck and resigned myself. *I have maybe five minutes to live. . .*

So many shades of beautiful green, the light, filtering through the leaves. Funny, as many times as I had been in the woods, I had never noticed all the colors . . . so beautiful. Now the light was turning golden. I thought, *It's a great evening to die.* And if I were going to choose a place, this tranquil spot deep in the woods was as good as any. I felt no pain, only acceptance.

I thought of Pam and our little son, Michael, and all the things I hadn't said, hadn't done for them. I'd always thought Pam deserved someone better than me. I was just a poor workingman; I had never accomplished anything important—and now I never would.

It occurred to me that my body would be hard to find out here; I had to try to get as far out of the woods as I could. I struggled over to the door, opened it, and climbed into the driver's seat.

I'd never made it out of the hollow with an empty truck; the hollow was so steep that you needed extra weight for traction. Then, when you got to the top, it was tricky—a hard turn, or you'd sail over the hill.

I stepped on the gas and roared up the slope, leaves spraying. I still don't know how, but I made it. Letting up on the gas just a bit, I started the turn, then hit the gas again, hard. The truck fishtailed between the trees, but moments later I was in a clearing.

Before me stretched a broad meadow. In the middle, about 350 yards away, was a huge old tree. *If I can make it there, it'll be far enough. They'll spot the truck.*

Away I went, jouncing and bouncing across that pasture. I bumped to a stop under the spreading canopy. I was still conscious but beginning to feel tired. Another couple of hundred yards farther, cows were grazing near a fence. On the other side of the fence was a road. Could

I make it there? I stepped on the gas again. Two minutes later I pulled up beside the fence and emerged from the truck. *This is pretty good,* I thought, *I made it this far.* The gate was made of heavy water pipe about seven feet long. And it opened uphill. Even if it had been unlocked I couldn't have opened it. I clambered over it.

By now, I felt as if I were walking underwater.

A car was coming up the hill. I wobbled toward it, waving my arms. The car slowed, but the driver must have thought I looked like a bloody scarecrow, because she stepped on the gas. I groaned.

I felt something warm on my chest. I looked down. Blood...

Up the road, perhaps one hundred feet away, was a boat-storage and tackle shop. Slowly, with great effort, I placed one foot ahead of the other, climbed the one big concrete step up onto the porch, and tottered to the door. It was dark inside.

Balling my fists, I banged on the windows. A light went on. Then, Peggy Suite, the proprietor, was staring at me through the glass.

Don't panic! Don't panic! I was thinking. I managed to croak, "Call an ambulance. . . ."

At once Peggy's partner, Dan, a bear of a man, was on the porch. He pulled a picnic bench from the wall and gently laid me on it. Then he went to fetch a towel. He pressed it hard against my neck. Quickly it soaked through.

"Am I dying?" I rasped.

"Now you just keep quiet!" Dan ordered. "You are not going to die."

"Pam...where's Pam?"

"She's coming. We've called the paramedics."

I felt a need for something...I wasn't sure what. I remembered a kindly Sunday school teacher who in my childhood had taken us fishing and told us stories about Jesus. But I never had use for religion and church—just more people telling me what to do.

"Dan...pray for me," I whispered.

"Uh, I don't know how," he replied awkwardly.

I was scared. I didn't know how to pray either. But I found myself talking to God. I told Him I was sorry I had lived the life I had and sorry for the things I'd done without knowing any better. "Please forgive me for my sins, God. Take my soul to heaven."

An incredible peacefulness roiled over me, and I no longer cared if I lived or died. Although the temperature was in the low thirties, a warmth flooded me from the inside out. I felt no pain.

"You know, God, this isn't fair at all," I said. "All my life I've gone my own way. And now, when I need You so bad and call out—there You are. I haven't done a thing to deserve this kind of love. I'm dying, I know. But if I had it to do over again, I would do it differently." I had an overpowering impression that God was listening—and approving.

I became aware that people were hovering, milling around me. A paramedic was leaning down, telling me to hold on. I was perplexed. *How come they're so upset?* I thought. *Can't they see how happy I am? It's okay. I'm so happy I'm glowing.*

My arms and legs began jerking with convulsions, but in my joy I hardly noticed or cared. Then hands were stripping my clothes away, putting canvas pressure leggings on me, carrying me to the ambulance. I looked up to see Pam beside me.

The ambulance did eighty all the way into Bloomington. The police had set up roadblocks all along our route. I was tired, so tired. By now I was drifting. Then, nothing.

The next morning the surgeon, Dr. James Topolgus, stopped by. I had lost 80 percent of my blood—as much as you can lose and live. But he had sewn me up and given me a transfusion. "You're very lucky I was on duty," he quipped. "You got the best care in town." He paused, and then said, "But I'm not that good."

People began stopping by my room at all hours, to see the guy who cut his throat and miraculously lived. And just five days after the accident I was feeling so much better that my doctor sent me home. Two months later I was back at work.

But now I was a changed man. I began devouring the Bible, learning all about this God Who had saved me. I began telling my story at Pam's church (which is now also mine), and at other local churches. I told my listeners I had always believed I was self-sufficient. That's why I loved being in the woods, my domain, where I thought I was in total control. But that cold October afternoon, I found out that I wasn't in control at all. God was. And when I acknowledged that, He reached down, held me—and saved me.

47.

Rain

by Dawn Adrian Adams

TODAY WAS MOVING DAY, BUT AS I STARED OUT THE WINDOW, SPATTERING DROPS OF GRAY RAIN TURNED INTO A HAMMERING DOWNPOUR.

It figures, I thought, fighting back the tears. It had been raining on the day my husband left me three months earlier, and as far as I was concerned, it had been raining ever since. I was in South Carolina, where we'd moved with our eight-year-old son, Harrison, a year before. I was more than a thousand miles away from my family, barely making ends meet, with bills piling up, fearful of the future without my husband.

At least I'd found a cheaper place for Harrison and me to live. We were moving out of the brick house we'd been renting and into a tiny three-room cottage about fifteen miles away at half the rent. To make the move, I'd borrowed a sorry old pickup truck from work. But I didn't have a tarp to cover our possessions that would go in the back of the truck. So I waited until the rain stopped, then told Harrison to hurry and help me load up.

Onto the truck went a wooden table and chairs, Harrison's bed and mattress, and a studio couch. I piled on cartons and wedged in the lamps.

Just then, the wind gusted up. Scanning the dark sky, I wanted to pray. When I was little, Daddy always said, "Make prayer a habit. Then, when there's an emergency and you need it most, praying will come naturally."

Now, though, the words stuck in my throat. I was still going to church, but I felt out of the fold. I'd prayed so hard for my marriage to be saved, but things just got worse, and I found it harder and harder to believe God could do anything.

Now, I thought bitterly, my belongings were about to get soaked. "Dear Lord," I said, "is it never going to stop raining on me?" I shoved the last box into the pickup and slammed the tailgate shut.

As we drove down the highway, the wind grew vicious. Twigs swirled against the windshield and the wind rattled the load stacked high in the back of the truck.

There was a *thunk.* In the rearview mirror I saw a chair toppling over against a floor lamp. Groaning, I pulled over, put the brake on, and let the engine idle while I stepped out and shoved the chair back in place.

The old truck coughed and stalled. I got back in and turned the key in the ignition. Nothing happened. I swallowed hard and tried again—and again. My fear and exhaustion were too much. I buried my face in my arms on the steering wheel.

I was surprised to feel my son grab my hand and squeeze it the way he'd always done when we'd prayed together. And I heard myself saying over and over, "Please, Lord, help us." I was doing what came naturally—praying. When I sat up, I felt more peaceful than I had felt in months.

I turned the ignition key. This time the engine started, and I pulled onto the highway. Ahead of us a dark curtain of rain stretched across the landscape.

"We're driving right into it, Mommy!" Harrison said.

The downpour came nearer and nearer. Now it was only two car-lengths ahead of us. Harrison and I braced for the hammering rain that would hit the truck at any minute.

Only it didn't. Harrison looked all around, then asked, puzzled, "Mommy, why don't we get to where the rain is?"

I was puzzled too. In the side and rearview mirrors I could see rain beating down alongside and in back of us. There was a curtain of rain on the fields to our right, and as we dipped between two small hills rain pelted a house and barn to our left as well. Every car that passed us had its lights on and sent up sheets of water—but I didn't even have to turn on our windshield wipers.

"Mommy," Harrison said, "it's raining everywhere but where we are!"

"Son," I said quietly, "I think God is going out of His way to let us know that it's stopped raining on us."

That night, after unloading our furniture and packing boxes, I tucked Harrison into bed. A sense of peace filled me. I no longer feared the future. Life's difficulties would not go away. But neither would God's presence and His love.

48.

Out of the Shadows
by Ellen Lawrence

I DID NOT WANT TO ATTEND THE ANNUAL FAMILY GATHERING AT HUNTING SEASON, BUT NONE OF MY USUAL EXCUSES WERE WORKING WITH KEN, MY HUSBAND OF FIVE MONTHS. I TRIED EXPLAINING MY AVERSION TO HUNTING: I COULDN'T BEAR THE SHOOTING OF WHAT I CALLED BAMBIES. WHEN THAT DIDN'T PERSUADE HIM, I COMPLAINED THAT I WAS JUST TOO BUSY WITH WORK. FINALLY I PULLED OUT ALL THE STOPS AND SAID, "I CONSIDER HUNTING AN ANCIENT CHAUVINISTIC RITUAL AND I DON'T WANT TO PARTICIPATE."

I did feel that way, but that wasn't the whole story. I couldn't tolerate even the thought of telling anyone why I really didn't want to go.

Each year around November 15 my family—aunts, uncles, cousins, and siblings—gathers under one roof up north near the town where I grew up. The location changes from year to year; this year it was to be held at my mother's home. I had not attended in more than twenty years; that's how long the secret had kept me away. But Ken was determined to go. It would help him get to know my family better, he said.

Snow was falling when we got there. My brothers hugged me and asked a dozen questions, which I answered mindlessly as I frantically looked around the family room for the uncle I feared might be there. He had not arrived.

Relaxing around a blazing fireplace, the men told funny, exaggerated stories about white-tailed deer that got away. The women planned meals, played board games, and laughed about "the savage hunters." Everyone had a favorite memory of past hunting seasons—everyone except me. At one point my eldest brother asked me, "Do you remember the year Dad wanted to take you hunting?"

Our father had been dead several years. For a moment that scene came back to me. I was thirteen and loved when my father took me along—anywhere. I remember his scratchy kisses and the sound of his laughter. His offer to take me along was a rite of passage. I was growing up.

But by that age I couldn't stand the thought of being with the men during hunting season. As much as I wanted to be with my father, opening day sent shivers up my back.

Now, as my sister, five brothers, and half a dozen other relatives recalled past hunting seasons, I stared at the driveway waiting for my uncle to arrive. Once again my secret was robbing me. I couldn't enjoy the time with my family.

Finally someone said the uncle wouldn't be joining us this year; his vision was just too bad. Yet even without his presence, the memories were too strong. I excused myself and went to bed early. But as I lay there in the dark, my eyes stubbornly open, I listened to every voice, every new arrival.

Next morning, in the predawn dimness of opening day, I watched Ken pull on his bright orange coat and straighten his hat. As he leaned down to kiss me before leaving, he said, "Is something wrong? You tossed and turned all night."

Looking past him at the wall, I said, "I guess it's just being in a strange bed." But even as I said it, I knew I was chained to something beyond my control. It was difficult for me to relax and to trust or give myself completely to anyone, even my husband—or God. A portion of my energy seemed permanently earmarked for protecting myself. And though I was a Christian and committed to my faith, I was afraid that if people knew what had happened, they would not want me or love me.

Opening day came and went. That night my exhausted husband fell asleep immediately, and two nights of not sleeping caught up with me. In my dreams, twenty years dissolved.

I was eleven years old. It was during hunting season, a time filled with the same noises and smells as now. I was sleeping on a cot in my aunt's house. It was a peaceful scene for a short moment. Then suddenly the room filled with swollen blue monsters circling the cot, many monsters, but each wore the same face: the face of one uncle. Each smelled of alcohol. Each wanted to touch me, hurt me.

When I shook myself awake, Ken was holding me, whispering that I was safe. I sat up, trembling, still sensing danger. My chest heaved as if I'd been wrestling. I felt cold and sweaty.

"I want to go home," I said, pulling away and rubbing at the tears on my cheeks. "I want to go home right now."

He smoothed my hair. "Now? You aren't serious."

"I'm leaving, Ken."

"I don't understand." He looked at me and noticed my quivering hands. His grip on my shoulders tightened. "Honey? Did you have a nightmare?"

I kept looking down. "I guess I did…yes."

"So tell me about it. Just talk about it; then it can't hurt you. It's over."

"There's nothing to tell you. I just want to leave. If you want to stay, you go ahead, but I'm leaving!" I threw the covers off, went to the closet, and pulled my suitcase out. In minutes I had stuffed my things into it and changed into sweats for the drive home. Ken sat in bed watching in disbelief. I tossed the suitcase onto the covers beside him and glared. "Well, are you staying or leaving?"

He shook his head. "This is insane. What are we going to tell your family? We can't just disappear."

I leaned closer. "I don't care what we tell them. I don't have to explain myself to anyone!"

Dear Lord, why did I agree to this? I thought. *What made me think I could come back here? Ken knows something is wrong. God, help me!*

But I couldn't tell him. I couldn't talk about something that might destroy me and everything that mattered in my life.

Now it was almost as if the secret had come out of its corner and was circling my feet, rubbing against me, threatening my sanity even as my husband looked at me with love and concern.

"Not anyone? Not me? Is this something you won't even talk to me about?" He sounded so hurt.

"There's no point in talking about this. It's old, it's the past. Talking won't help. I just want to leave."

"It won't go away," he said, climbing out of bed. "If it's this upsetting, it isn't going to vanish when we drive south." He reached for his shirt.

I wrote my mother a vague note about not feeling well, then we left. But as we traveled farther and farther from that place, my memory didn't slither back to its assigned spot in the shadows. It stood in the early hints of dawning light that streaked the sky over pine trees, taunting me.

Ken glanced at me from time to time. I leaned my head against the window, and tears started down my face. The memory seemed almost real. . . .

I saw my uncle's face. I felt his hands on me. I felt the brush of his red hunting coat. The cot in my memory toppled over and I was pinned to the tile floor. I felt the terror of not understanding what was happening or how an uncle I'd adored could do this to me. I smelled his breath, reeking of alcohol. Helpless to stop the scene in my mind, I watched as my uncle raped my childhood and left me crying in the dark on the morning of opening day.

When Ken pulled off the road, it was a shattered child he held and comforted. The flashback left me drained. I shut my eyes and rested in Ken's arms. Clinging together, we sat silent for a long time. I had not told the secret yet, but it seemed to dare me to tell. I knew I could submerge it again. That would make it go away for a while. But I also knew it would be back. It would remain my master. . . .

Ken kissed my wet cheeks. He looked confused, scared. "Honey, if you don't talk about this, it's going to eat you up inside. It will be a wall between us. You need to tell someone. If you can't tell me, we'll find someone you can tell. I wish it could be me."

If ever a person said all the right things at just the right time, it was my husband at that critical moment. So there at the side of the road, I told the secret.

And it didn't destroy me—or my marriage. When I finished, Ken cried too, and in his eyes I saw acceptance. All those years I had been afraid that no one who knew my secret could ever truly love me, not even God. Now that it was out, though, I felt more loved than I had ever thought I could be.

As Ken pulled back onto the road, the sun was just coming up over the hills to the southeast, pushing back the shadows around the tall pines and flooding the snow-covered landscape with light. It was one of the most glorious sights I had ever seen. It was almost as if God Himself was telling me, "The secret's power over you is broken."

And so it was. My healing had begun.

49.

The Choice
by Ruth Vaughn

MY BROTHER JOE STOOD BESIDE MY OPEN COFFIN, GRANITE-FACED IN SORROW. HIS WIFE, FRANCES, SAT ON A FALLEN LOG NEARBY, HER HUNCHED SHOULDERS SHAKING. LYING IN MY CASKET IN MORGAN MILL CEMETERY, WHERE GENERATIONS OF MY FAMILY LAY BURIED, I LOOKED UP AT JOE AND FRANCES, GRATEFUL TO KNOW THEY CARED SO MUCH. THEY WOULD MISS ME, I KNEW, BUT THEY WOULD BE ALL RIGHT.

My choice was clear: life or death. And I knew what I wanted. Deliberately, I reached up to pull the casket lid down. After all the suffering, all the sorrow, I would be free of pain at last.

But as the opening narrowed to just inches, I stopped. I gasped. *What on earth have I been thinking? My sons. They still need me!*

I threw the lid open, sat up, and found myself staring directly into the face of my doctor. "You've been in a coma for three days," he said, telling me I'd had a toxic reaction to my sleep medication.

I looked around, trying to get my bearings. Though my vision was blurry, out of focus, I could identify the narrow hospital bed, the IV dripping. "Toxic reactions to this drug," my doctor explained, "can include visual disruptions, coma, and for some, death."

I dared not speak. I hardly trusted myself to move. For the reality my doctor was describing was so totally different from the equally vivid world I had just left behind, a world where I had fought and won battles, a world where I had only moments ago chosen life over death.

A nurse came in to consult with the doctor about another patient. I noticed a poinsettia on my dressing table, a tiny Christmas tree, a couple of festively wrapped gifts. Oh yes. It was December.

After the nurse left, the doctor studied my chart. "Everything's under control," he said. "You've survived and your vision should be normal within a few days. But prepare yourself for tonight. You probably won't sleep. Your system has to cleanse out the toxicity, and because of the drug, I can't give you any sleep medication."

As my eyes followed him out the door, I found myself half-expecting the door to open again to admit a blond, blue-eyed, smiling man, the man who had been my rock and my comfort during each of my many hospital stays during our thirty years of marriage. Part of me knew, knew for certain, that he would not come. Yet my heart didn't believe that at all.

It all still seemed so impossible. I always knew I might get cancer. That was a possibility. I always knew I might fall into an earthquake crack. That was a possibility. Even Addison's disease, which had robbed my body of hormones, sapped me of my strength, and reduced me to skin and bones. That was a possibility. But there was one thing that I'd thought would never happen to me: divorce. That was not how I loved. My marriage was too sacred, divorce unthinkable.

Nonetheless, he was gone.

I was alone.

For the first time in my life, that December, I was having to face a hospital crisis without a loving husband present.

Night brought other patients merciful sleep, but not me. As the night wore on, my body became more and more agitated until eventually my arms were flopping around, hopelessly out of control.

But far greater than the physical distress was the emotional anguish. The one person who had vowed to honor and cherish me in sickness and in health had proved faithless. Throughout this long night, except for the nurse who periodically checked on me, the flickering light of the television would be my only companion. *He's gone,*

Ruth, the motionless door seemed to shout every time I glanced at it. *Gone, and never coming back.*

Ever since the divorce I felt like one of those spiral shells washed up on a beach. Poke a toothpick in and around, you find nothing there. Was a life like that worth living?

Only hours before, in another reality, God had offered me a choice. Had I lowered my casket lid only a few inches more, my suffering would have been all over by now. I felt sure of it. Now I was wondering, had I made the wrong choice?

In my coma world I had fought for my boys and won. I had been in a boxing ring, arms coiled, fists clenched. From the sidelines I had heard Ronnie and Billy cheering me on. "You'll win, Mom. You'll win for us." And I knew I would. I always had. That's what a mother does.

It was for my boys that I had chosen life. But through that tormented night I wondered: Even if I am alive for my boys, in my condition—sick, confined, dependent—what use will I be to them?

Why, God? I cried silently into the darkness. *Why won't You work a miracle to make the world all right again?* I must have asked Him a hundred questions.

And God was silent.

I was totally alone.

Hour after sleepless hour, I hurled accusations and demanded explanations. Yet as much as I wanted God to explain, there was something I wanted more, much more. I needed to know there was a God Who knew my name, Who knew my need, Who knew me. A God Who cared for me, one small woman in Presbyterian Hospital in Oklahoma City.

When at long last pastel streaks began erasing the night's blackness, my despair only deepened. I didn't want another day to come! My lifelong belief in a loving God was teetering. This notion of omnipotence caring for one fragile, frail human heart—was it all only wishful thinking? During that long night I had found no reassurance that my faith was rooted in fact.

During that next day, and the next, and the next, I saw no such evidence. If God really cared, why didn't He show me?

Then came the morning when the doctor decided I should put my legs to the test. Trembling, they held me upright and, haltingly, shakily, moved me forward. The doctor grinned and invited me to take a walk in the hall.

I pulled my blue chenille robe on over my hospital gown, stepped into slippers, and eased out the door. After my days in a coma world filled with events as vivid as any I have ever known, I had begun to wonder: Had I been hallucinating? I had feared I might be in the psychiatric ward. Now I read with relief the sign on the door:

Ruth Vaughn Endocrinology

I walked the empty corridor on unsteady legs. From a closed room I could hear a voice. "Sweet little Jesus boy..." it sang, but I hardly noticed, and kept on moving. Then suddenly a phrase in the song stopped me cold: "We didn't know who You was."

It was only a husky voice on television, only a Christmas carol in December, but inside an empty shell, a new life began to stir.

Oh, God, I see it now. I wasn't hallucinating. You were there in that boxing ring, giving me the strength to fight. In the coffin too, You were there, giving me the choice of living or dying—then reminding me of my two boys who needed me.

But as the lyric floated through the door, enfolding me, I realized that the same God Who had allowed me to choose to live or die had also compressed Himself into human flesh, to suffer and die, so I would know that in my suffering I am never alone.

As I walked on down the hall, the words of the spiritual followed me: "But please, Sir, forgive us, Lord... We didn't know 'twas You."

50.

At the End of a Rainbow
by Beverly Thompson

AS A CHILD GROWING UP IN EASTERN WASHINGTON STATE, RAIN-
BOWS WERE ALWAYS A WONDER TO ME. OFTEN I WOULD RUN AS
FAST AS I COULD ACROSS THE PASTURE OF MY UNCLE'S FARM TO
FIND THE RAINBOW'S END—BUT IT ALWAYS VANISHED BEFORE
ME.

After I married, my life was spent on Washington's west coast,
where the rainfall was heavy and on many days I might see two or
three rainbows at the same time. In Aberdeen, they fell into forests,
and in Seattle, they dropped behind tall, gray buildings in the next city
block. And I always was tempted to run to the corner and peek, just to
see if maybe . . . Near our home in Enumclaw, my children and I chased
a rainbow in the car for three miles because it looked as if its end lay
just ahead of us. Not so. In time, I tired of chasing rainbows.

Then came a rainy week in early spring when word came that one
of my son Jim's third-grade classmates had died of leukemia. As Jim
and I drove back from the funeral, I was troubled and confused. There
didn't seem to be any answers to my son's questions or my own. Why
did little boys have to die? And where was God when they did?

As we drove up the bluff along the Chehalis River, the rain stopped and the sun broke through the clouds. Not one, not two, but four rainbows arched across the sky, brilliant and beautiful! And, wonder of wonders, the largest of them rose from the river, spread up, up over the bluff, and poured down to cover the highway ahead of us. We were driving straight into it!

Suddenly the inside of our car was filled with light. Jim and I were bathed in luminous colors—violet, azure, green, yellow, rose—and we marveled at them and gloried in them. Then, just as suddenly, they were gone. I looked into the rearview mirror and saw the cars behind me transformed by light as one by one they passed through the spectrum.

What had happened? I felt different, refreshed, new. My despair and confusion were gone, and in their place I felt peace.

In Genesis 9:13, the Lord said, "I do set My bow in the cloud, and it shall be for a token of a covenant between Me and the earth." That rainbow had reminded me of His covenant, His promise that He would be there to watch over us. Now, no matter what, I must just trust Him. At last, I had found the end of a rainbow, and in it God's covenant of caring shone brighter than gold.

A Note from the Editors

We hope you enjoy *Love, Mercy & Grace*, created by the Books and Inspirational Media Division of Guideposts, a nonprofit organization that touches millions of lives every day through products and services that inspire, encourage, help you grow in your faith, and celebrate God's love in every aspect of your daily life.

Thank you for making a difference with your purchase of this book, which helps fund our many outreach programs to military personnel, prisons, hospitals, nursing homes, and educational institutions. To learn more, visit GuidepostsFoundation.org.

We also maintain many useful and uplifting online resources. Visit Guideposts.org to read true stories of hope and inspiration, access OurPrayer network, sign up for free newsletters, download free e-books, join our Facebook community, and follow our stimulating blogs.

To learn about other Guideposts publications, including the best-selling devotional *Daily Guideposts*, go to ShopGuideposts.org, call (800) 932-2145, or write to Guideposts, PO Box 5815, Harlan, Iowa 51593.